I REMEMBER BEIRUT

STORY AND ART BY ZEINA ABIRACHED
TRANSLATION BY EDWARD GAUVIN

FIRST AMERICAN EDITION PUBLISHED IN 2014 BY GRAPHIC UNIVERSE™.
PUBLISHED BY ARRANGEMENT WITH ÉDITIONS CAMBOURAKIS.

I REMEMBER BEIRUT
©2008 ÉDITIONS CAMBOURAKIS
ENGLISH TRANSLATION COPYRIGHT ©2014 BY LERNER PUBLISHING GROUP, INC.

MAP ON PAGE 5 ©LAURA WESTLUND/INDEPENDENT PICTURE SERVICE.

GRAPHIC UNIVERSE™ IS A TRADEMARK OF LERNER PUBLISHING GROUP, INC.

GRAPHIC UNIVERSE™
A DIVISION OF LERNER PUBLISHING GROUP, INC.
241 FIRST AVENUE NORTH
MINNEAPOLIS, MN 55401 USA

FOR READING LEVELS AND MORE INFORMATION, LOOK UP THIS TITLE AT
WWW.LERNERBOOKS.COM.

LIBRARY OF CONGRESS CATALOGING-IN-PUBLICATION DATA
ABIRACHED, ZEINA, 1981-
    I REMEMBER BEIRUT / WRITTEN BY ZEINA ABIRACHED ; ART BY ZEINA ABIRACHED ;
  TRANSLATION BY EDWARD GAUVIN.
      P.   CM
    ISBN 978-1-4677-3822-4 (LIB. BDG. : ALK. PAPER)
    ISBN 978-1-4677-4660-1 (EBOOK)
    1. ABIRACHED, ZEINA, 1981- —JUVENILE LITERATURE. 2. BEIRUT (LEBANON)—
  BIOGRAPHY—JUVENILE LITERATURE. 3. LEBANON—HISTORY—20TH CENTURY—JUVENILE
  LITERATURE. 4. ABIRACHED, ZEINA, 1981-—COMIC BOOKS, STRIPS, ETC. 5. BEIRUT
  (LEBANON)—BIOGRAPHY—COMIC BOOKS, STRIPS, ETC. 6. LEBANON—HISTORY—20TH
  CENTURY—COMIC BOOKS, STRIPS, ETC. 7. GRAPHIC NOVELS. I. TITLE.
  DS87.2.A333A3 2014
  741.5'95692—DC23   2013047112

MANUFACTURED IN THE UNITED STATES OF AMERICA
1 - PC - 7/15/14

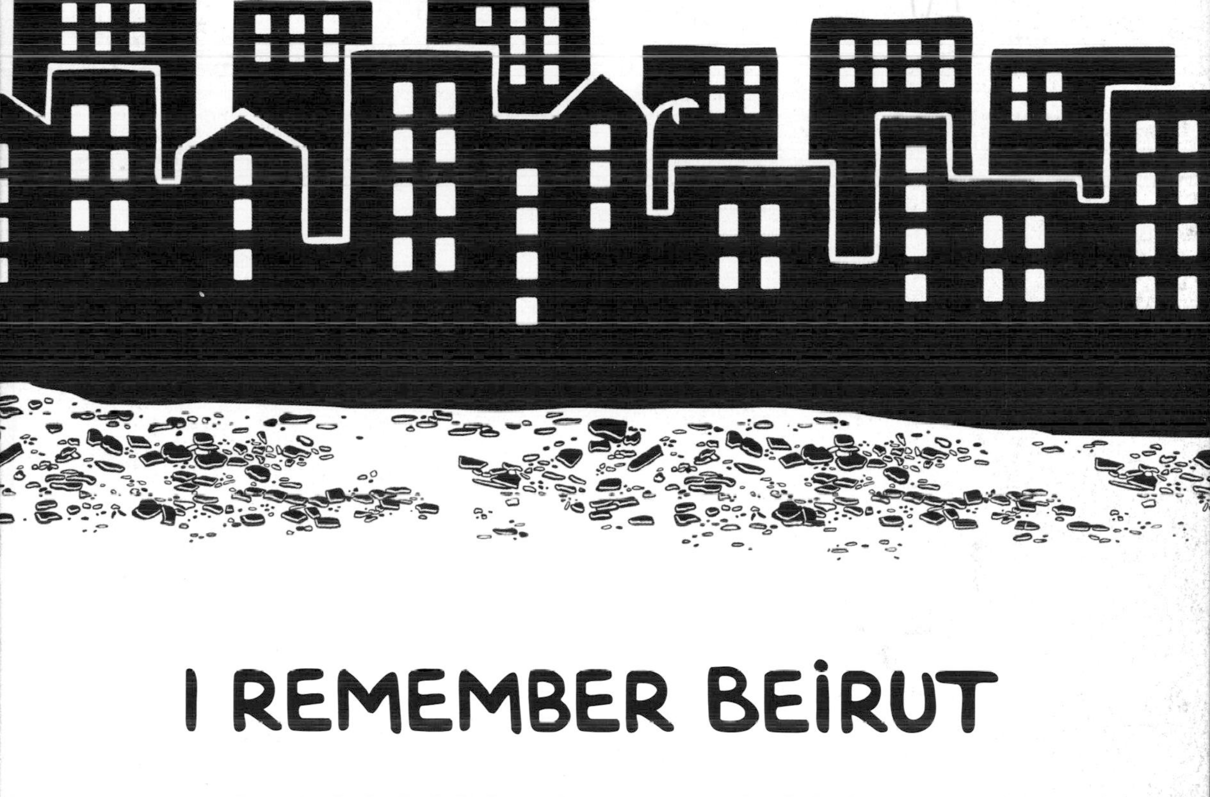

I REMEMBER BEIRUT

ZEINA ABIRACHED

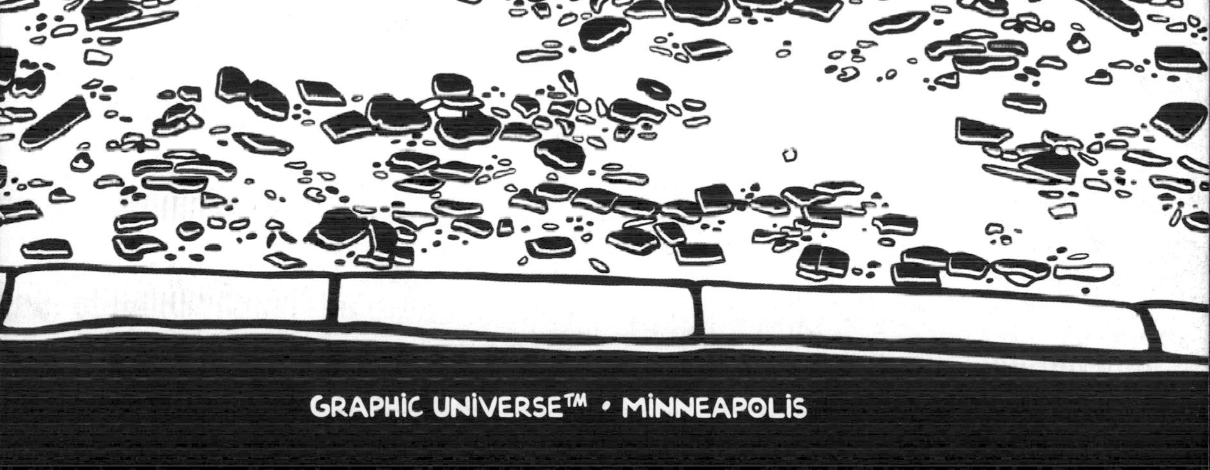

GRAPHIC UNIVERSE™ • MINNEAPOLIS

iNTRODUCTiON

The Lebanese Civil War lasted from 1975 to 1990. The conflict
began when fighting broke out between the Christians of Lebanon
and an alliance of Lebanese Muslims and Palestinian refugees.
Over time, some groups of Christian and Muslim combatants
also began to fight among themselves. Multiple outside countries
became involved in efforts to restore order. For many years, the
fighting divided Lebanon's capital city, Beirut. Zeina Abirached
was born in the middle of the civil war, in 1981.

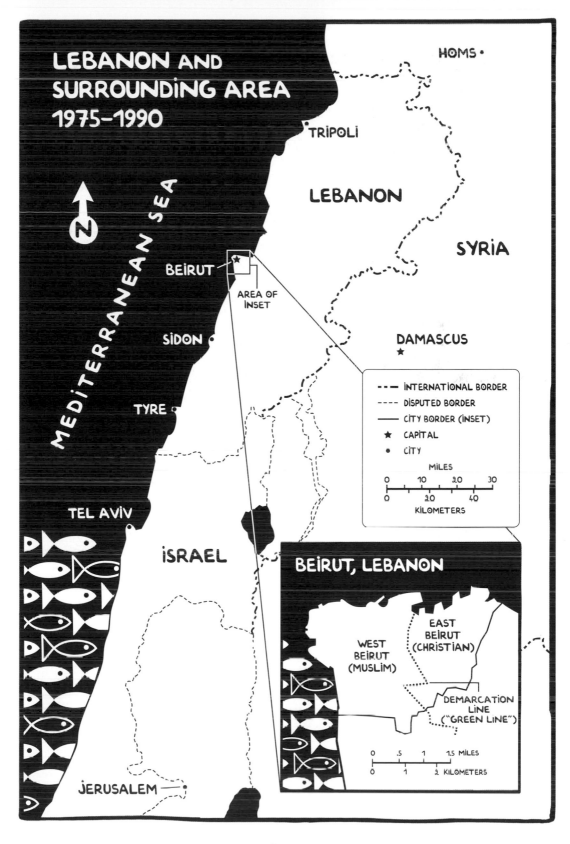

LEBANON AND SURROUNDING AREA 1975–1990

HOMS •

TRIPOLI •

LEBANON

SYRIA

N

MEDITERRANEAN SEA

BEIRUT ⊠★

AREA OF INSET

SIDON ∘

DAMASCUS ★

TYRE ∘

INTERNATIONAL BORDER
DISPUTED BORDER
CITY BORDER (INSET)
★ CAPITAL
• CITY

MILES
0   10   20   30
0   20   40
KILOMETERS

TEL AVIV •

ISRAEL

BEIRUT, LEBANON

WEST BEIRUT (MUSLIM)

EAST BEIRUT (CHRISTIAN)

DEMARCATION LINE ("GREEN LINE")

0   .5   1   1.5 MILES
0   1   2 KILOMETERS

JERUSALEM — •

"NOTHING DISTINGUISHES
MEMORIES FROM ORDINARY
MOMENTS. ONLY LATER DO
THEY MAKE THEMSELVES
KNOWN, FROM THEIR SCARS."

—CHRIS MARKER

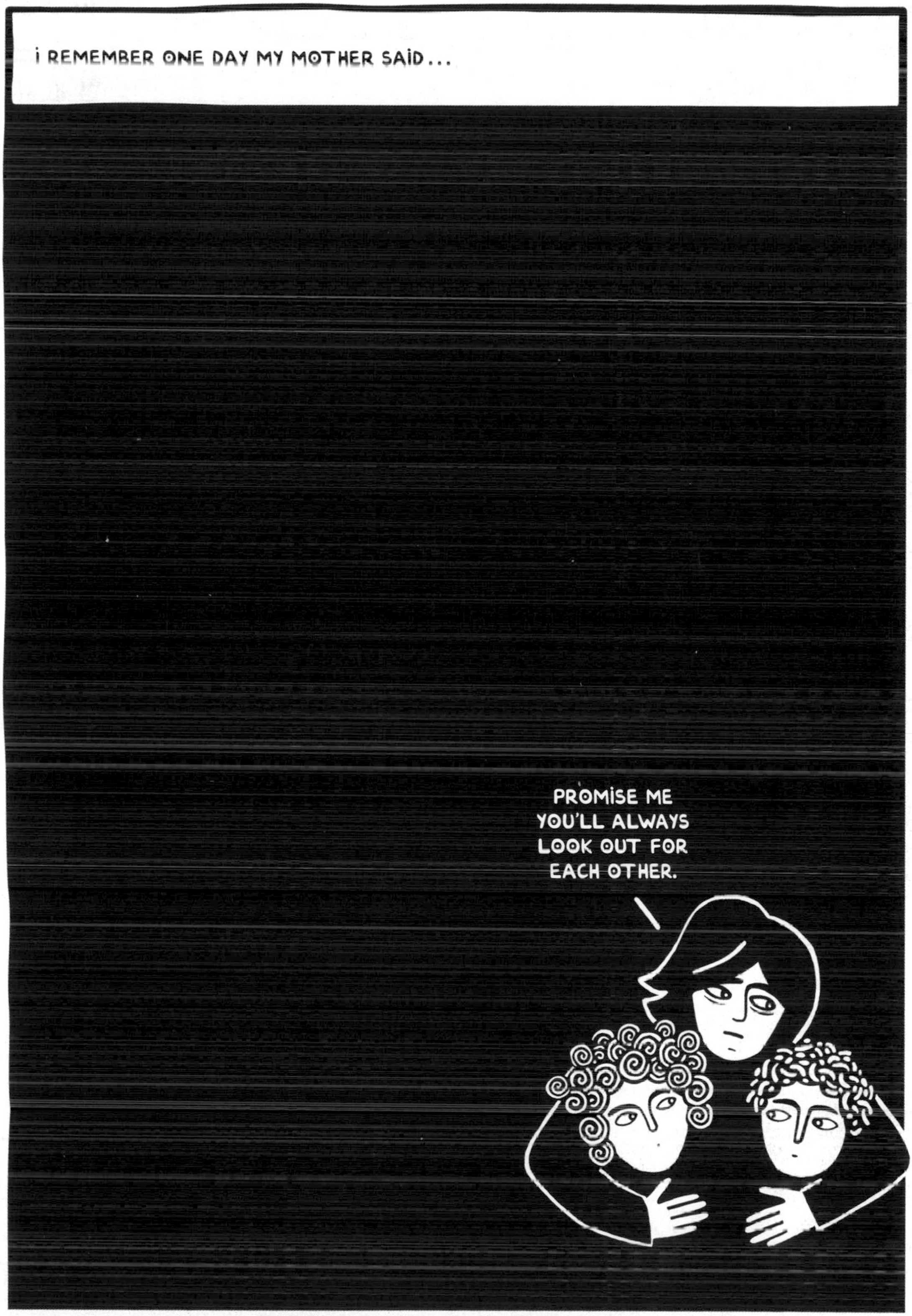
i REMEMBER ONE DAY MY MOTHER SAiD...
PROMiSE ME YOU'LL ALWAYS LOOK OUT FOR EACH OTHER.

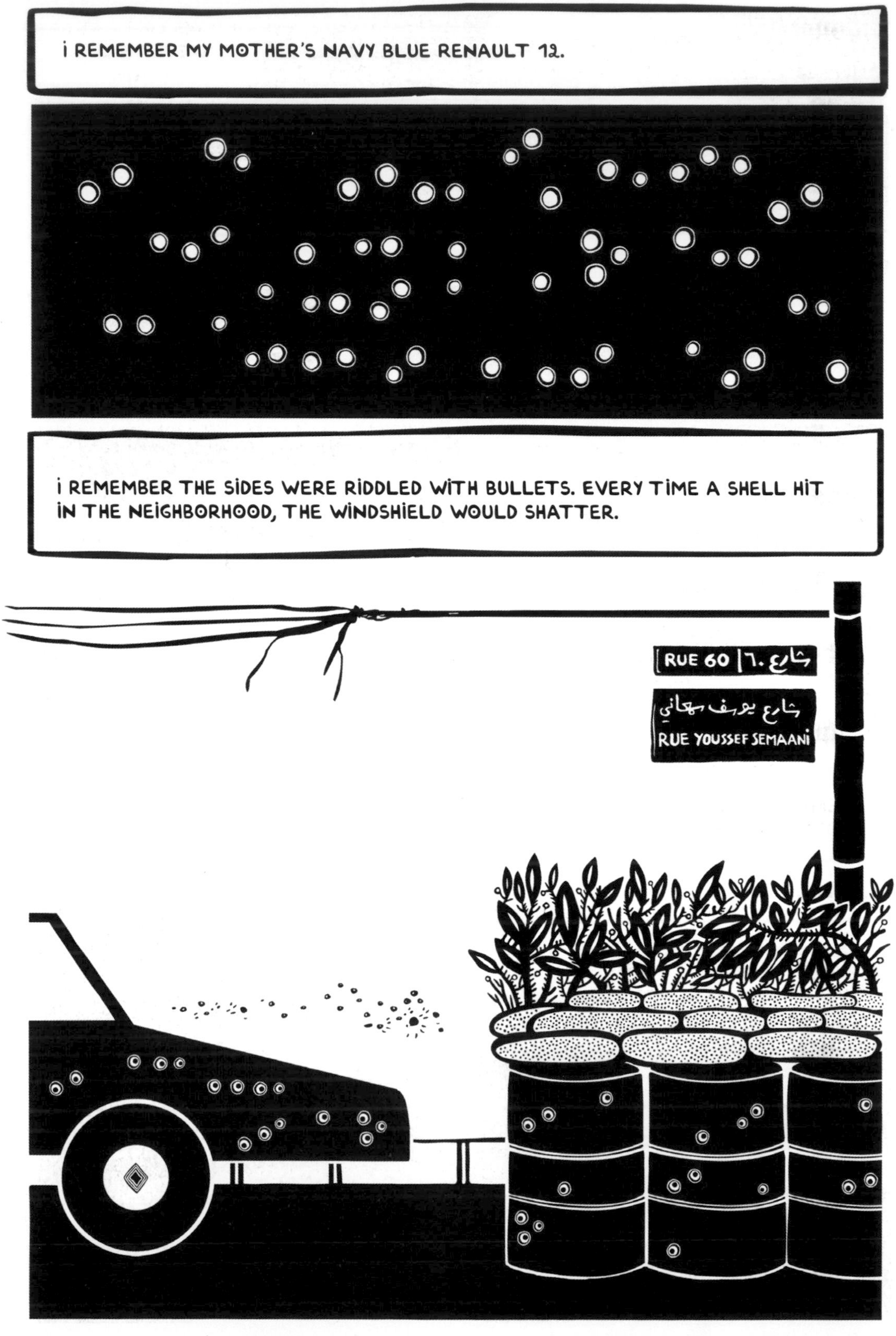
I REMEMBER MY MOTHER'S NAVY BLUE RENAULT 12.
I REMEMBER THE SIDES WERE RIDDLED WITH BULLETS. EVERY TIME A SHELL HIT IN THE NEIGHBORHOOD, THE WINDSHIELD WOULD SHATTER.
RUE 60 | شارع ٦٠
RUE YOUSSEF SEMAANI

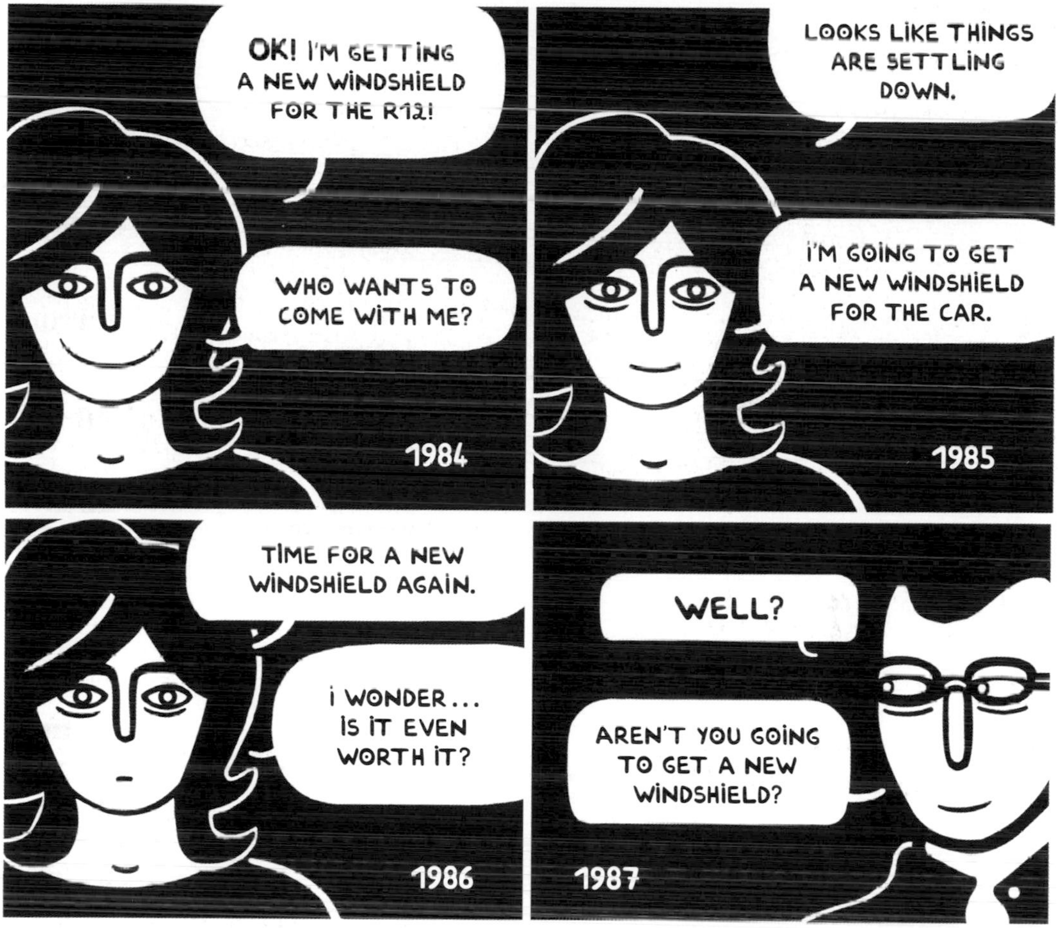
OK! I'M GETTING A NEW WINDSHIELD FOR THE R12!
WHO WANTS TO COME WITH ME?
1984
LOOKS LIKE THINGS ARE SETTLING DOWN.
I'M GOING TO GET A NEW WINDSHIELD FOR THE CAR.
1985
TIME FOR A NEW WINDSHIELD AGAIN.
I WONDER... IS IT EVEN WORTH IT?
1986
WELL?
AREN'T YOU GOING TO GET A NEW WINDSHIELD?
1987

I REMEMBER THAT AFTER A WHILE, MY MOTHER GOT SICK OF REPLACING THE WINDSHIELD ON HER R12. SHE WOULD WEAR SUNGLASSES WHEN SHE DROVE, TO SHIELD HER EYES.

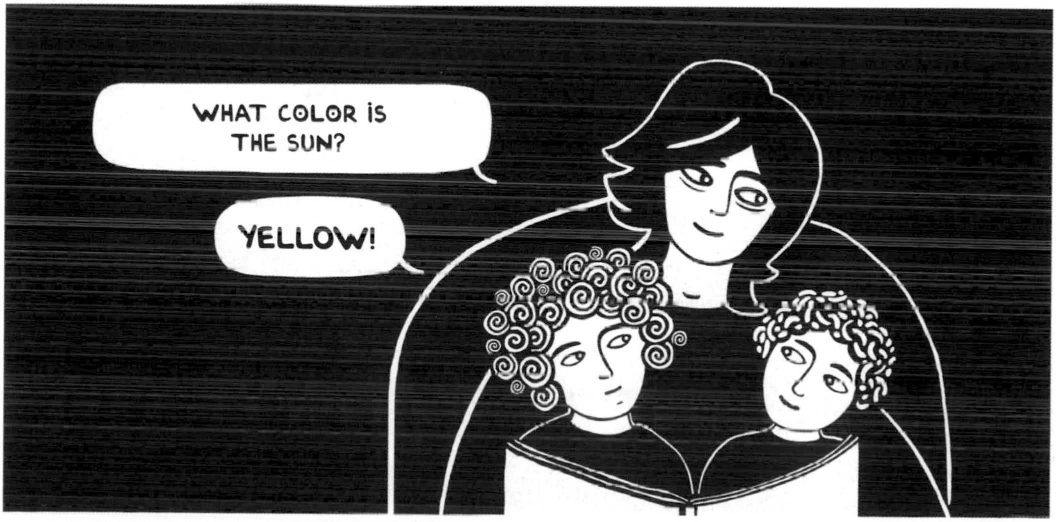
WHAT COLOR IS THE SUN?
YELLOW!

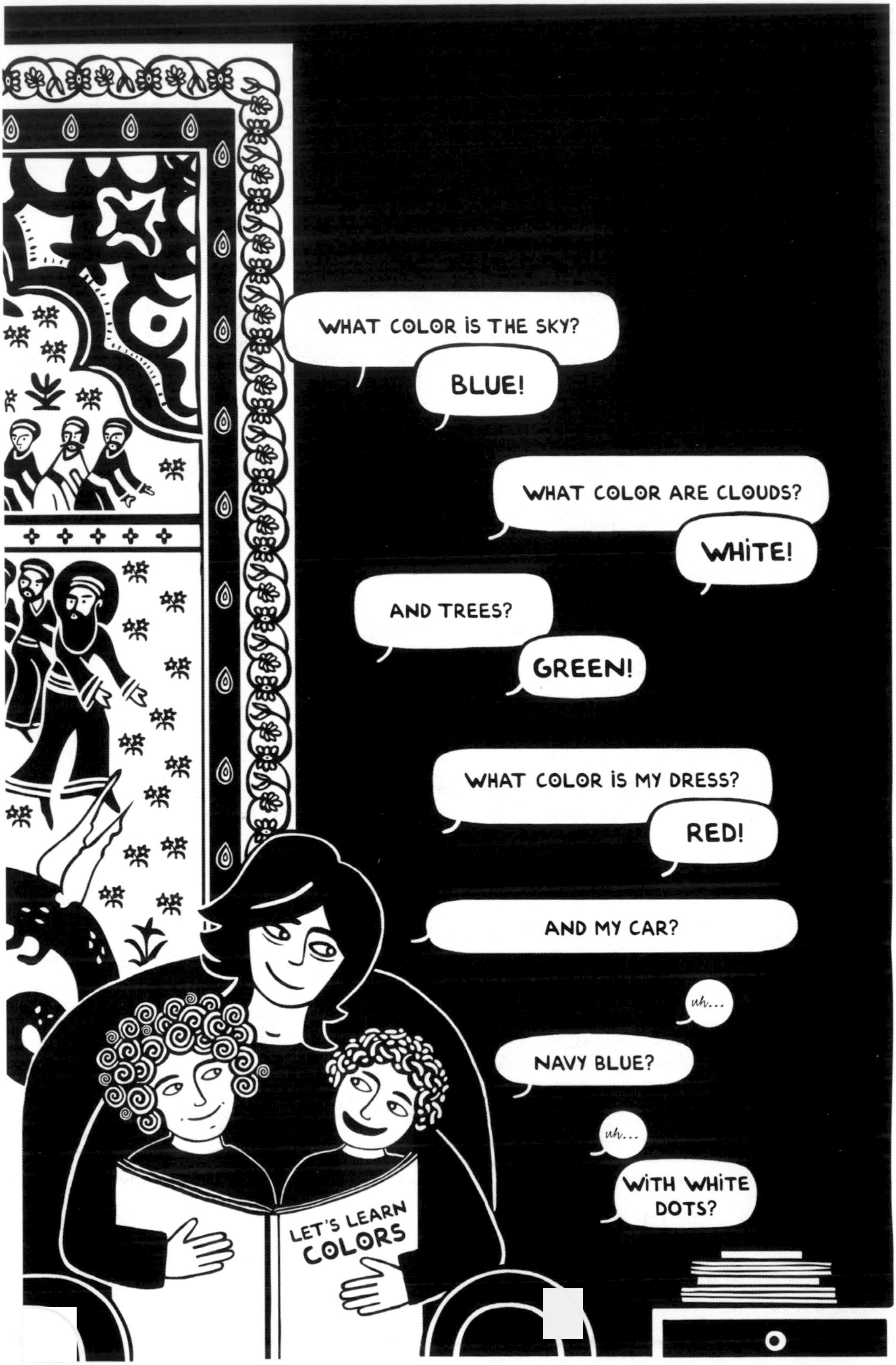
WHAT COLOR IS THE SKY?
BLUE!
WHAT COLOR ARE CLOUDS?
WHITE!
AND TREES?
GREEN!
WHAT COLOR IS MY DRESS?
RED!
AND MY CAR?
uh...
NAVY BLUE?
uh...
WITH WHITE DOTS?
LET'S LEARN COLORS

I REMEMBER THAT DURING THE WAR, THE SCHOOL BUS SKIPPED OUR NEIGHBORHOOD. THE NEIGHBORHOOD'S ALLEYS WERE CLOSE TO THE DEMARCATION LINE AND HAD A DANGEROUS REPUTATION.

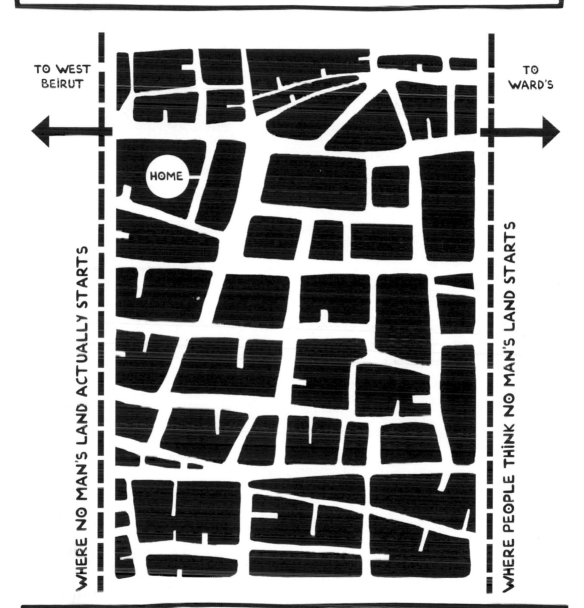

TO WEST BEIRUT

TO WARD'S

HOME

WHERE NO MAN'S LAND ACTUALLY STARTS

WHERE PEOPLE THINK NO MAN'S LAND STARTS

THE BUS WOULD STOP AT WARD'S ICE CREAM PARLOR AT 6:30 EVERY MORNING AND 3:30 EVERY AFTERNOON.

BY VIRTUE OF BEING ON THE EDGE OF THE ZONE WHERE THE BUS DIDN'T DARE GO, WARD'S HAD BEEN TURNED INTO A BUS STOP.

AT FIRST, THE PARENTS IN OUR NEIGHBORHOOD TOOK TURNS DRIVING KIDS TO WARD'S IN THE MORNING AND PICKING THEM UP IN THE AFTERNOON.

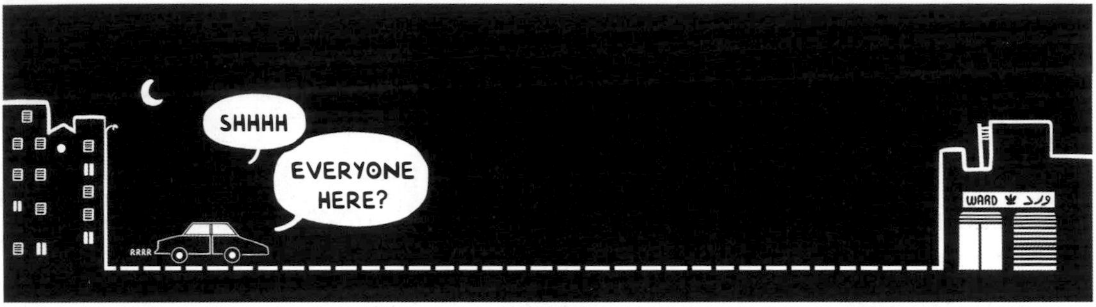

SHHHH
EVERYONE HERE?
RRRR
WARD ورد

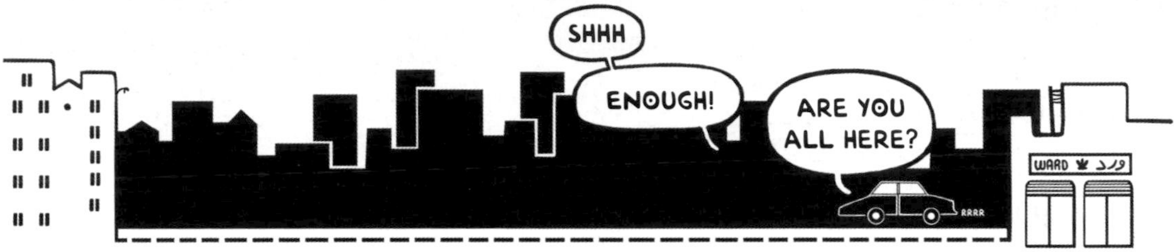

SHHH
ENOUGH!
ARE YOU ALL HERE?
RRRR
WARD ورد

THEN THEY ENTRUSTED THIS THANKLESS TASK TO MR. GEORGE.

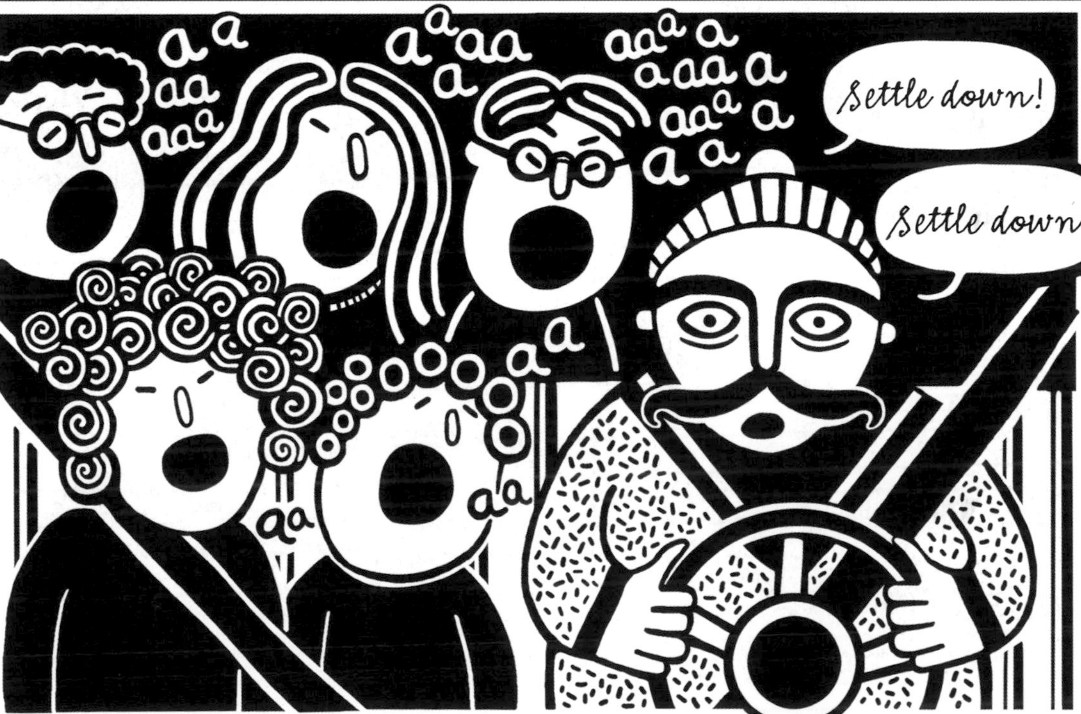

Settle down!
Settle down!

MR. GEORGE WAS A TAXI DRIVER. HE HAD A HUGE CAR EVERYONE CALLED "THE BOAT." HE ALWAYS PARKED IT AT THE INTERSECTION OF LEBANON STREET AND ST. JOSEPH UNIVERSITY STREET. WE COULD ALWAYS FIND HIM STANDING NEXT TO THE CAR, LOOKING FOR HIS NEXT FARE.

…INSHA'ALLAH!

…TO DRIVE ON THE STREETS OF BEIRUT, JUST

FOURTEEN YEARS LATER, HE TAUGHT ME TO DRIVE ON THE STREETS OF BEIRUT, JUST BEFORE I GOT MY LICENSE.

my right foot braking instinctively

SLOW DOWN!

SLOW DOWN!

YEE-HAW!

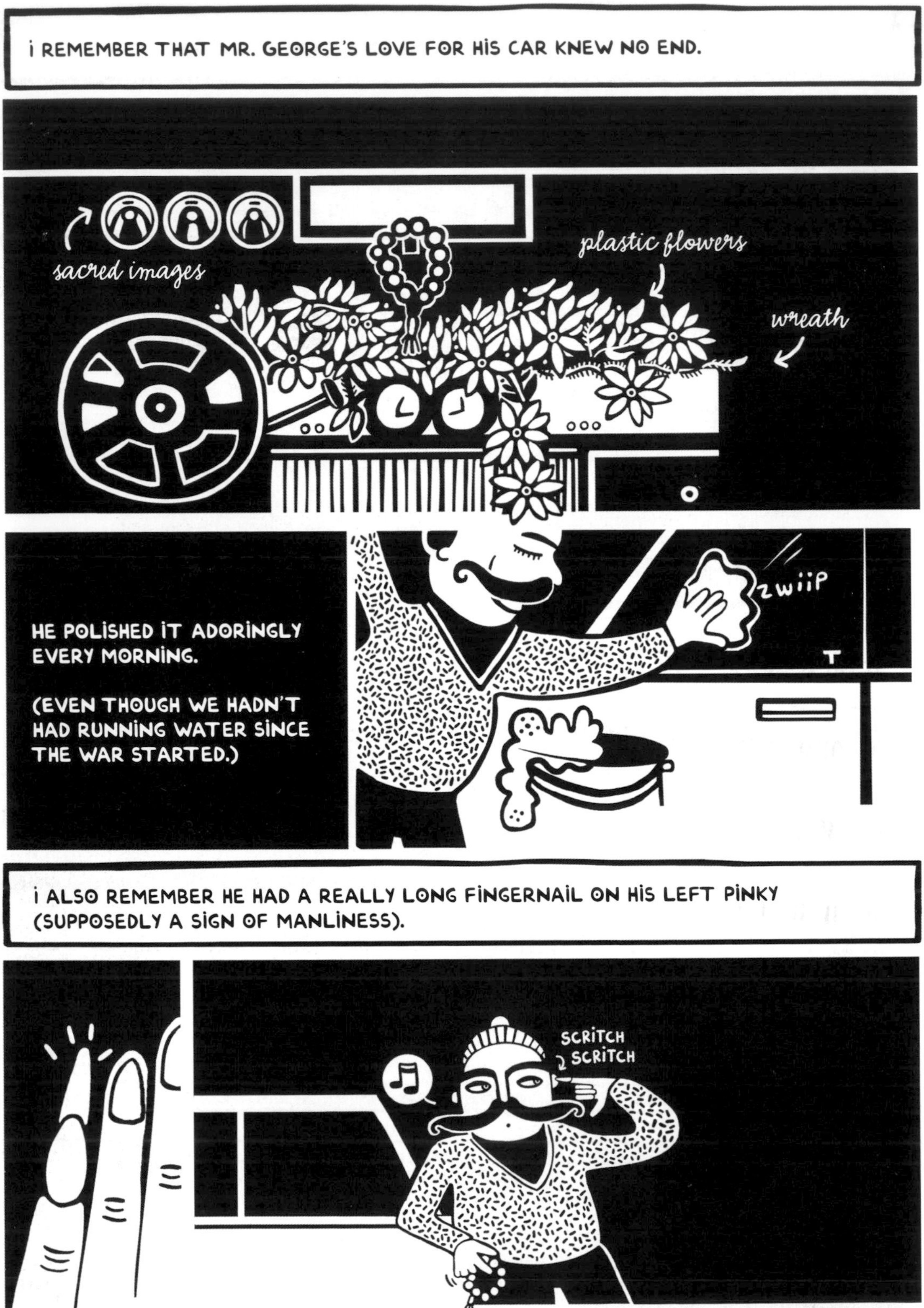
I REMEMBER THAT MR. GEORGE'S LOVE FOR HIS CAR KNEW NO END.
sacred images
plastic flowers
wreath
HE POLISHED IT ADORINGLY EVERY MORNING.
(EVEN THOUGH WE HADN'T HAD RUNNING WATER SINCE THE WAR STARTED.)
zwiip
I ALSO REMEMBER HE HAD A REALLY LONG FINGERNAIL ON HIS LEFT PINKY (SUPPOSEDLY A SIGN OF MANLINESS).
SCRITCH SCRITCH

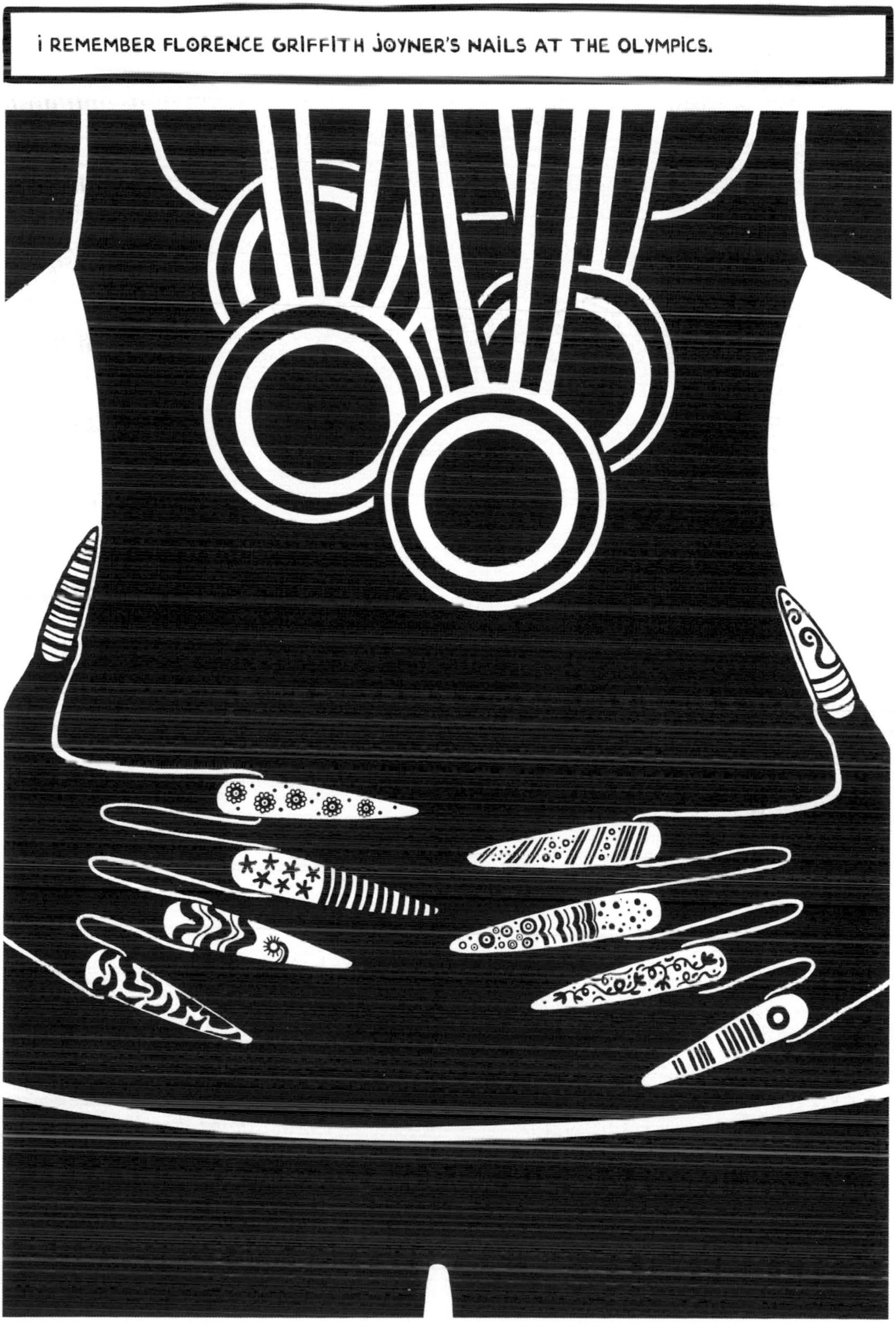
i REMEMBER FLORENCE GRIFFITH JOYNER'S NAILS AT THE OLYMPICS.

I REMEMBER GIANT ROBOT CARTOONS.

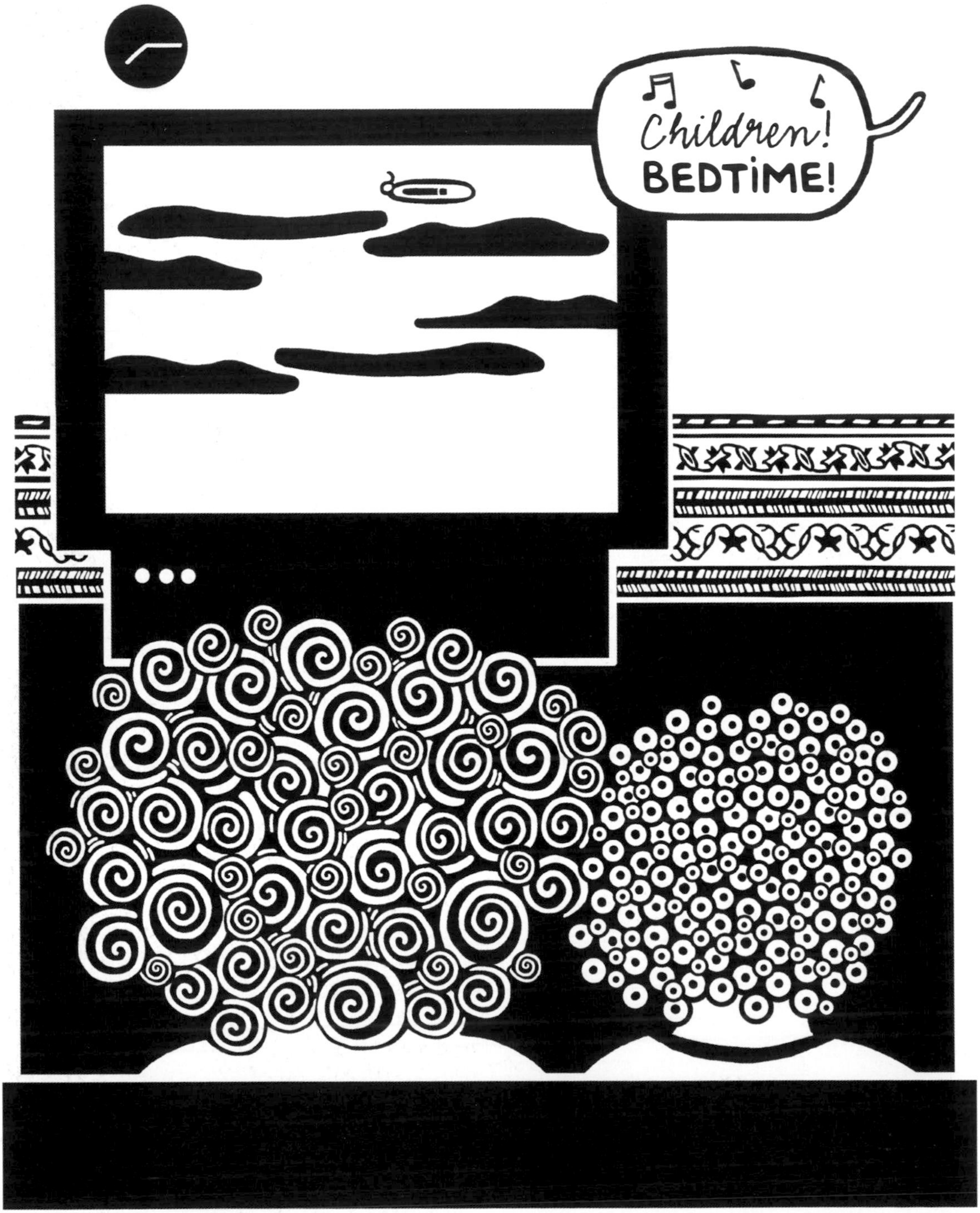
Children! BEDTIME!

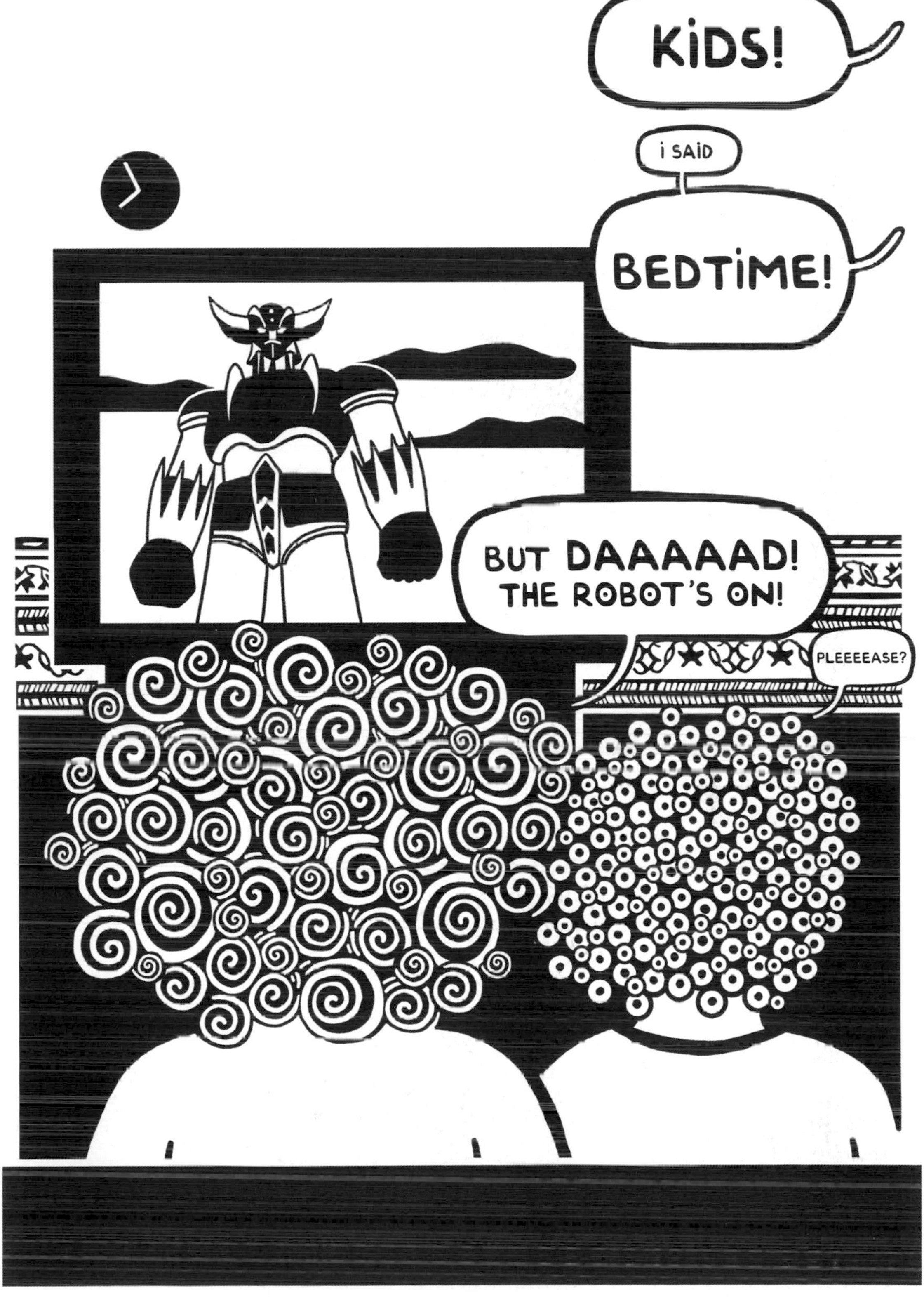
KIDS!
I SAID
BEDTIME!
BUT DAAAAAD! THE ROBOT'S ON!
PLEEEEASE?

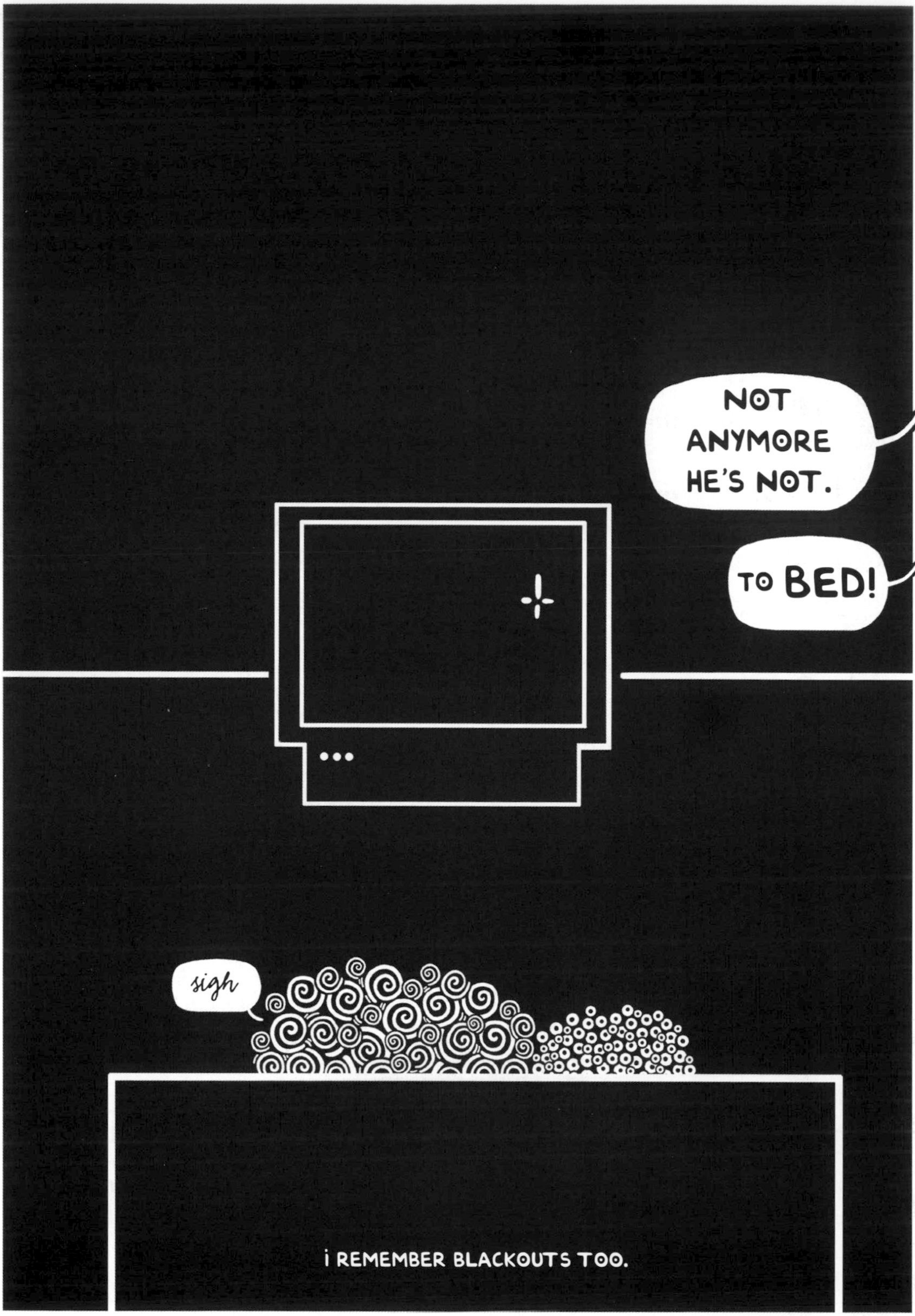
NOT ANYMORE HE'S NOT.
TO BED!
sigh
i REMEMBER BLACKOUTS TOO.

I REMEMBER WHEN THERE WAS NO ELECTRICITY OR GAS, WE USED KEROSENE FOR HEATING.

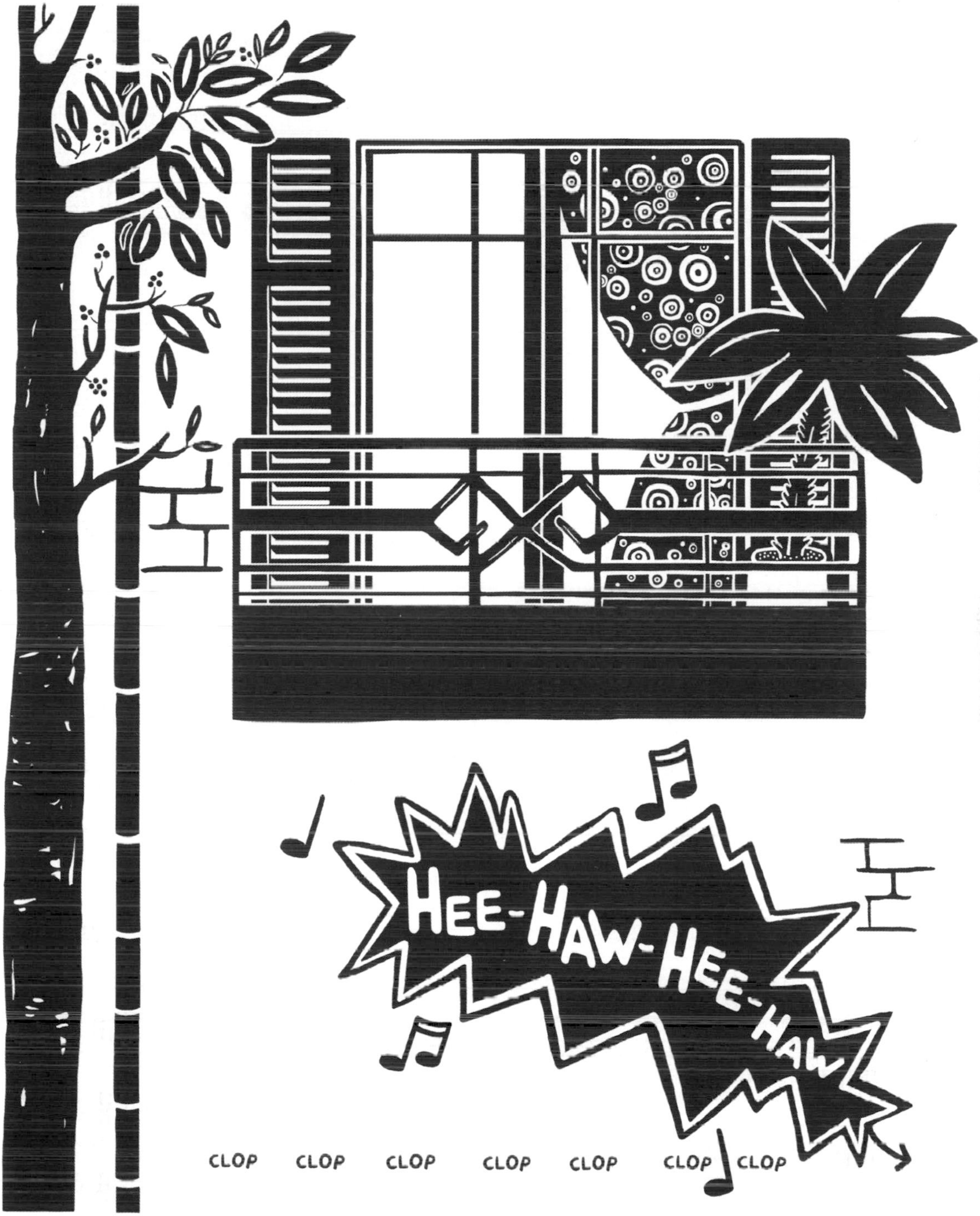
HEE-HAW-HEE-HAW
CLOP CLOP CLOP CLOP CLOP CLOP CLOP

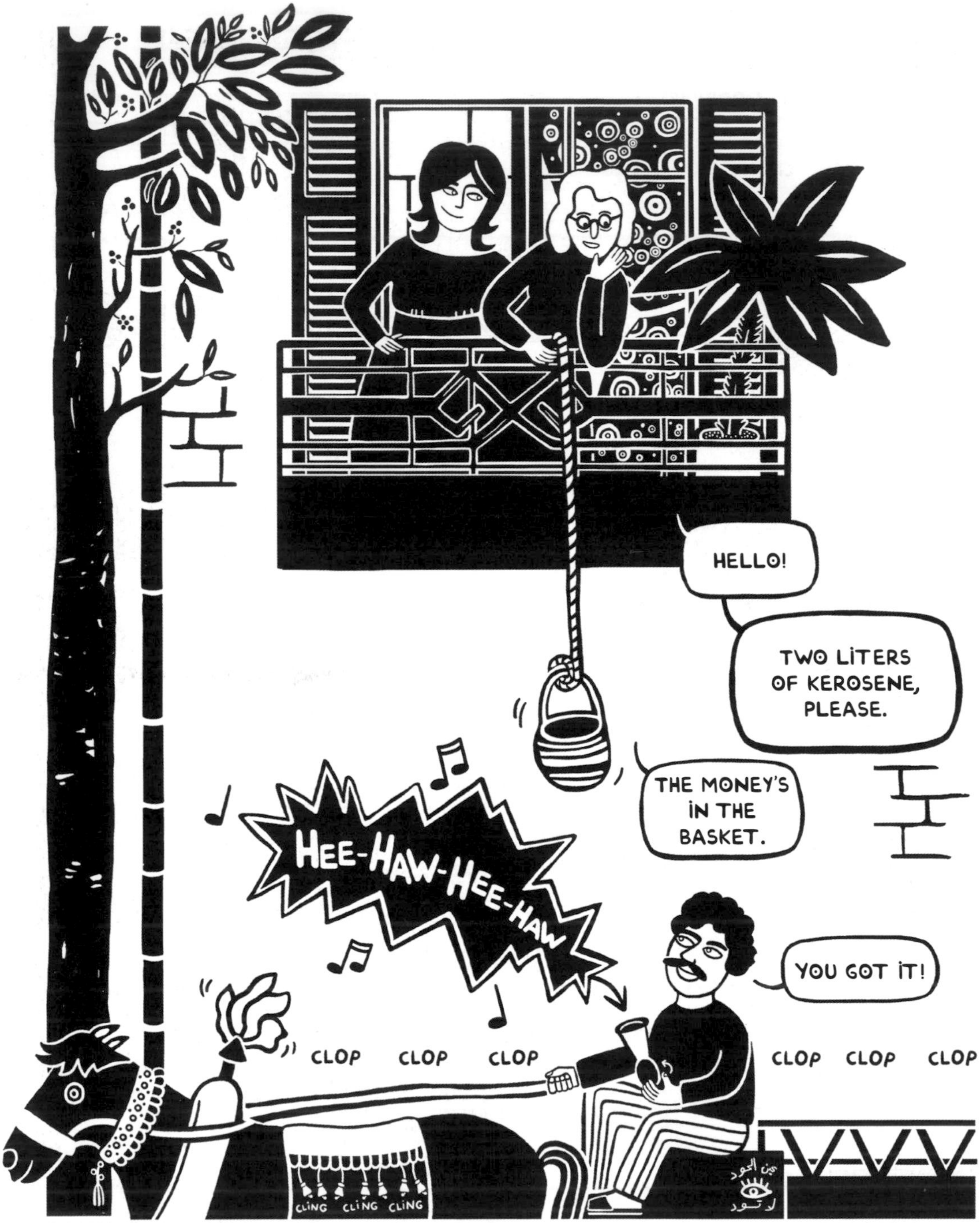
HELLO!
TWO LITERS OF KEROSENE, PLEASE.
THE MONEY'S IN THE BASKET.
HEE-HAW-HEE-HAW
YOU GOT IT!
CLOP CLOP CLOP
CLOP CLOP CLOP
CLING CLING CLING

THE GAS MAN WOULD ROAM THE NEIGHBORHOOD WITH A TANK ON A LITTLE HORSE-DRAWN CART.

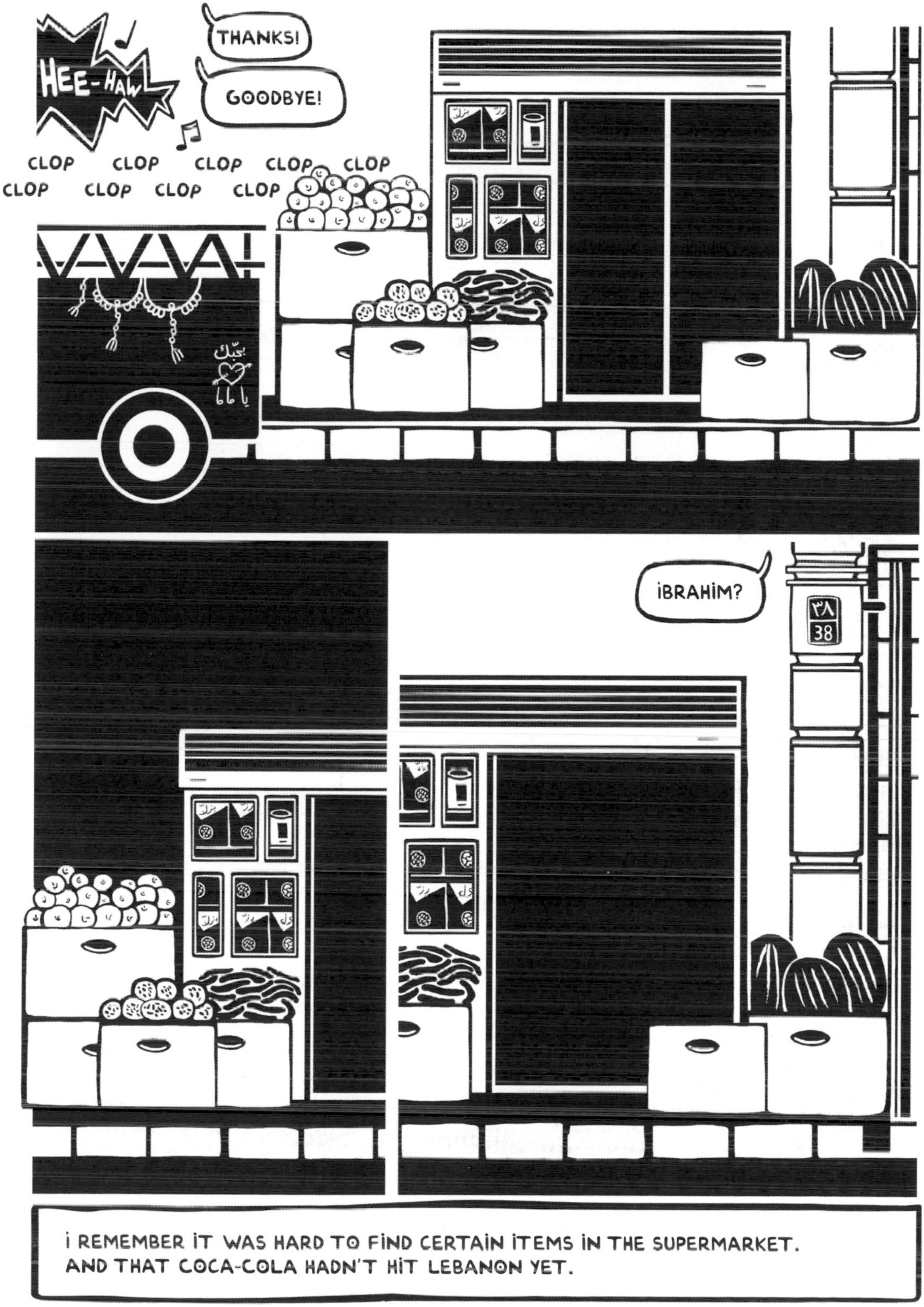
HEE-HAW
THANKS!
GOODBYE!
CLOP CLOP CLOP CLOP CLOP
CLOP CLOP CLOP CLOP
İBRAHİM?
٣٨
38
İ REMEMBER İT WAS HARD TO FİND CERTAİN İTEMS İN THE SUPERMARKET.
AND THAT COCA-COLA HADN'T HİT LEBANON YET.

I REMEMBER WE BOUGHT RC COLA IN GLASS BOTTLES, THEN GAVE THE EMPTIES BACK TO THE GROCER.

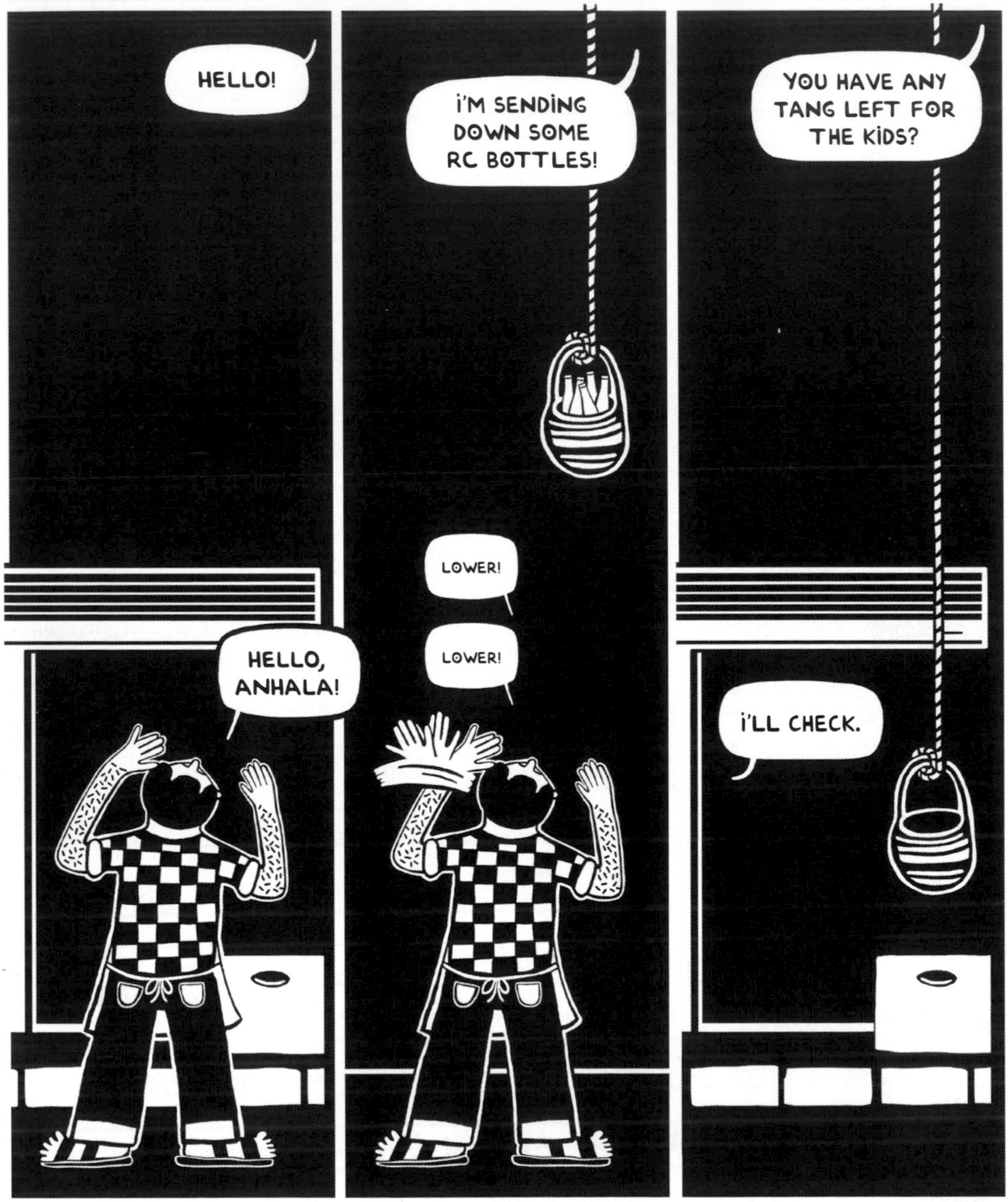
HELLO!
HELLO, ANHALA!
I'M SENDING DOWN SOME RC BOTTLES!
LOWER!
LOWER!
YOU HAVE ANY TANG LEFT FOR THE KIDS?
I'LL CHECK.

I REMEMBER TANG TOO!

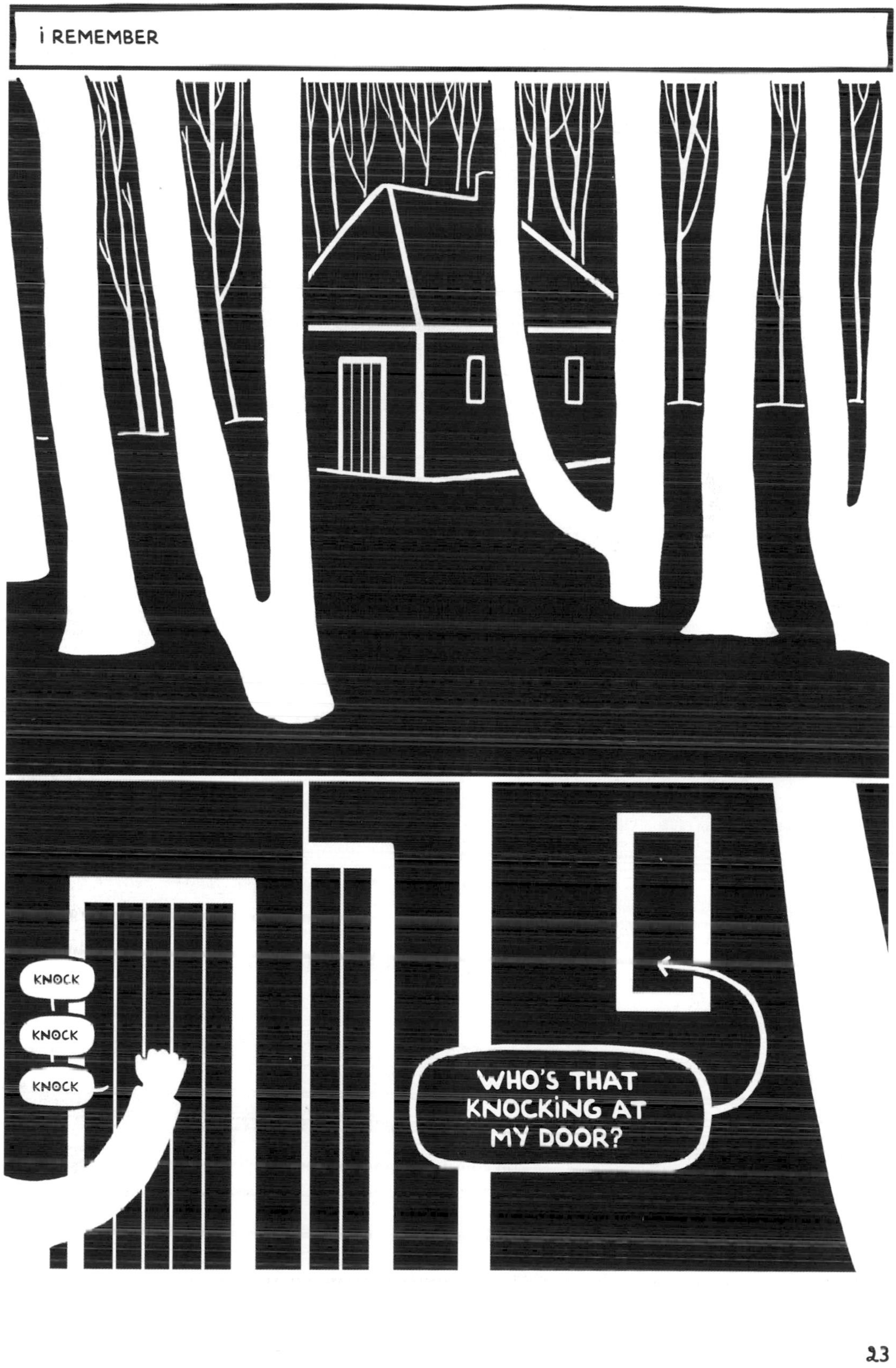
i REMEMBER
KNOCK
KNOCK
KNOCK
WHO'S THAT KNOCKiNG AT MY DOOR?

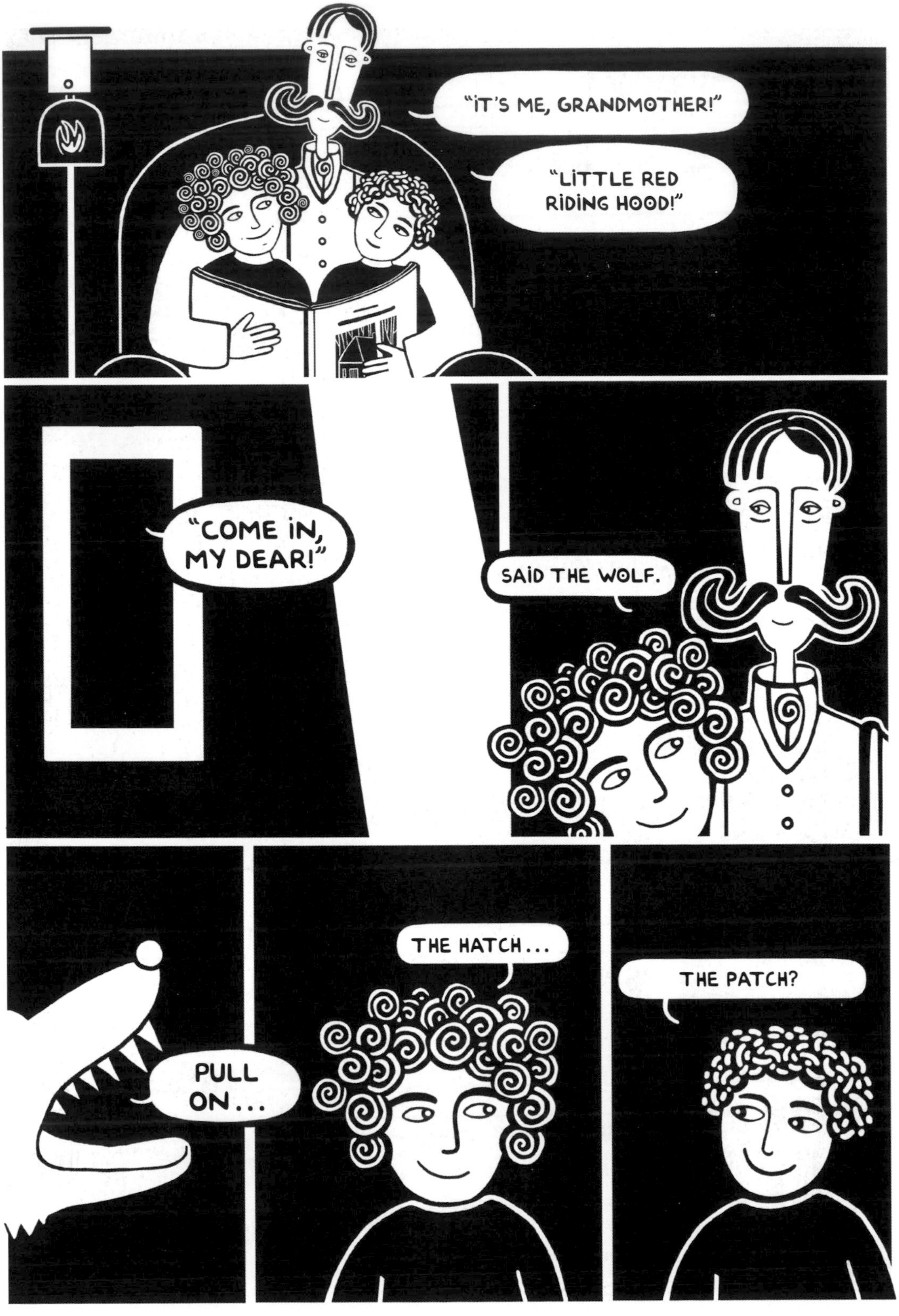
"IT'S ME, GRANDMOTHER!"
"LITTLE RED RIDING HOOD!"
"COME IN, MY DEAR!"
SAID THE WOLF.
PULL ON...
THE HATCH...
THE PATCH?

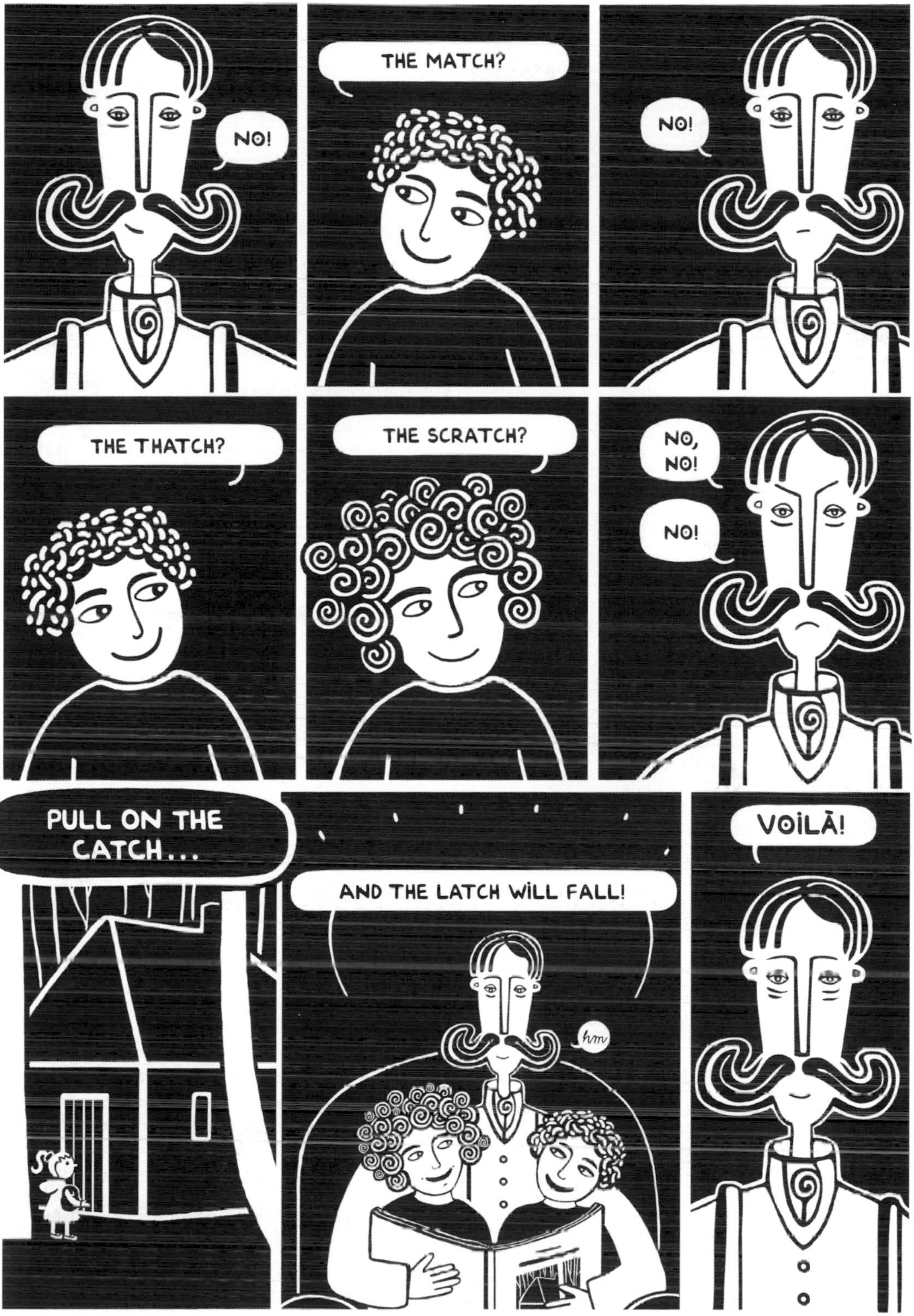
NO!
THE MATCH?
NO!
THE THATCH?
THE SCRATCH?
NO, NO!
NO!
PULL ON THE CATCH...
AND THE LATCH WILL FALL!
hm
VOILÀ!

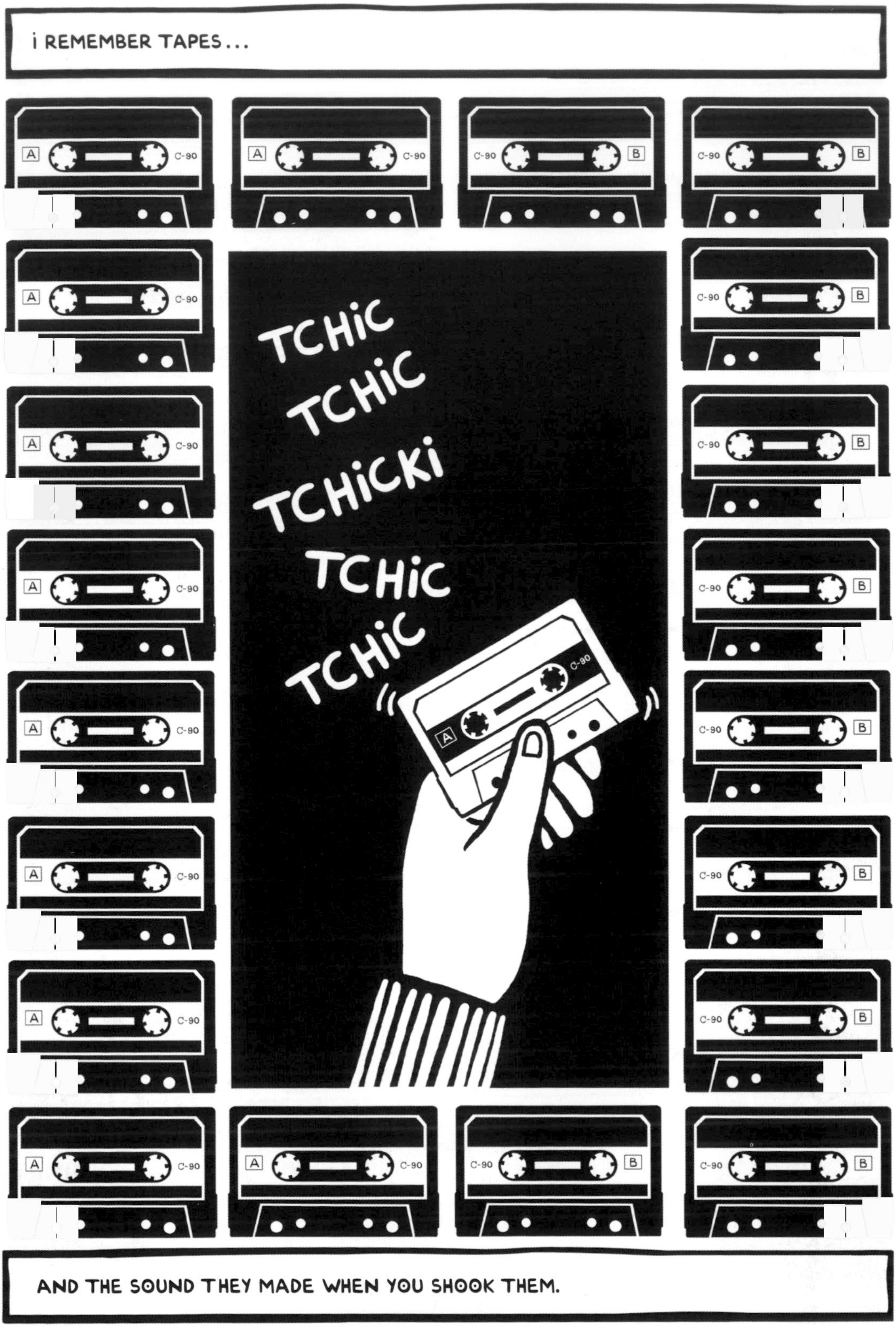
i REMEMBER TAPES...
TCHiC
TCHiC
TCHiCKi
TCHiC
TCHiC
AND THE SOUND THEY MADE WHEN YOU SHOOK THEM.

I REMEMBER SABAH.
AND THE CLIP FROM HER SONG "AYYAM EL LOULOU."

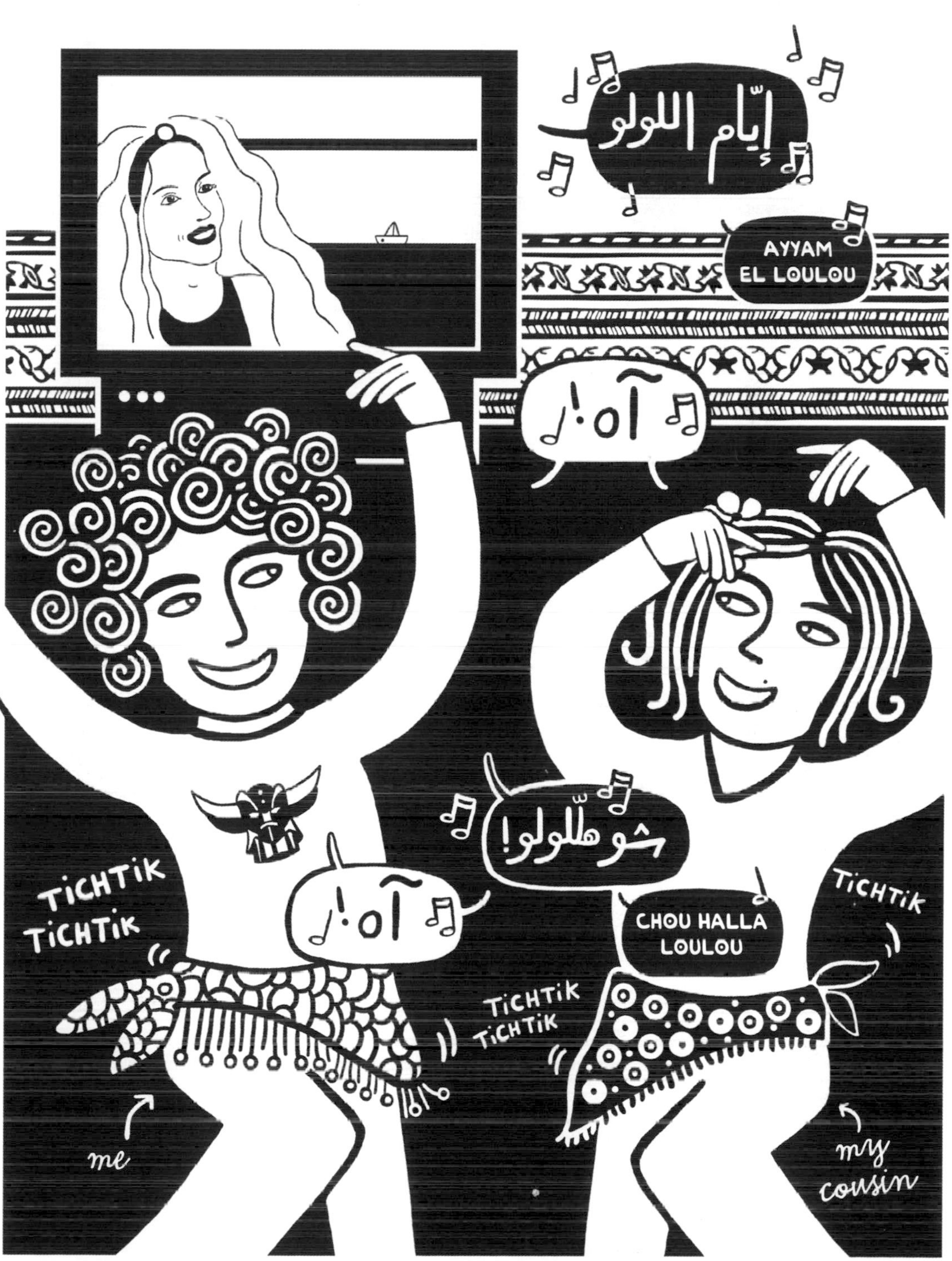
إيّام اللولو
AYYAM EL LOULOU
آه!
TICHTIK TICHTIK
آه!
شو هلّلولو!
CHOU HALLA LOULOU
TICHTIK
TICHTIK TICHTIK
me
my cousin

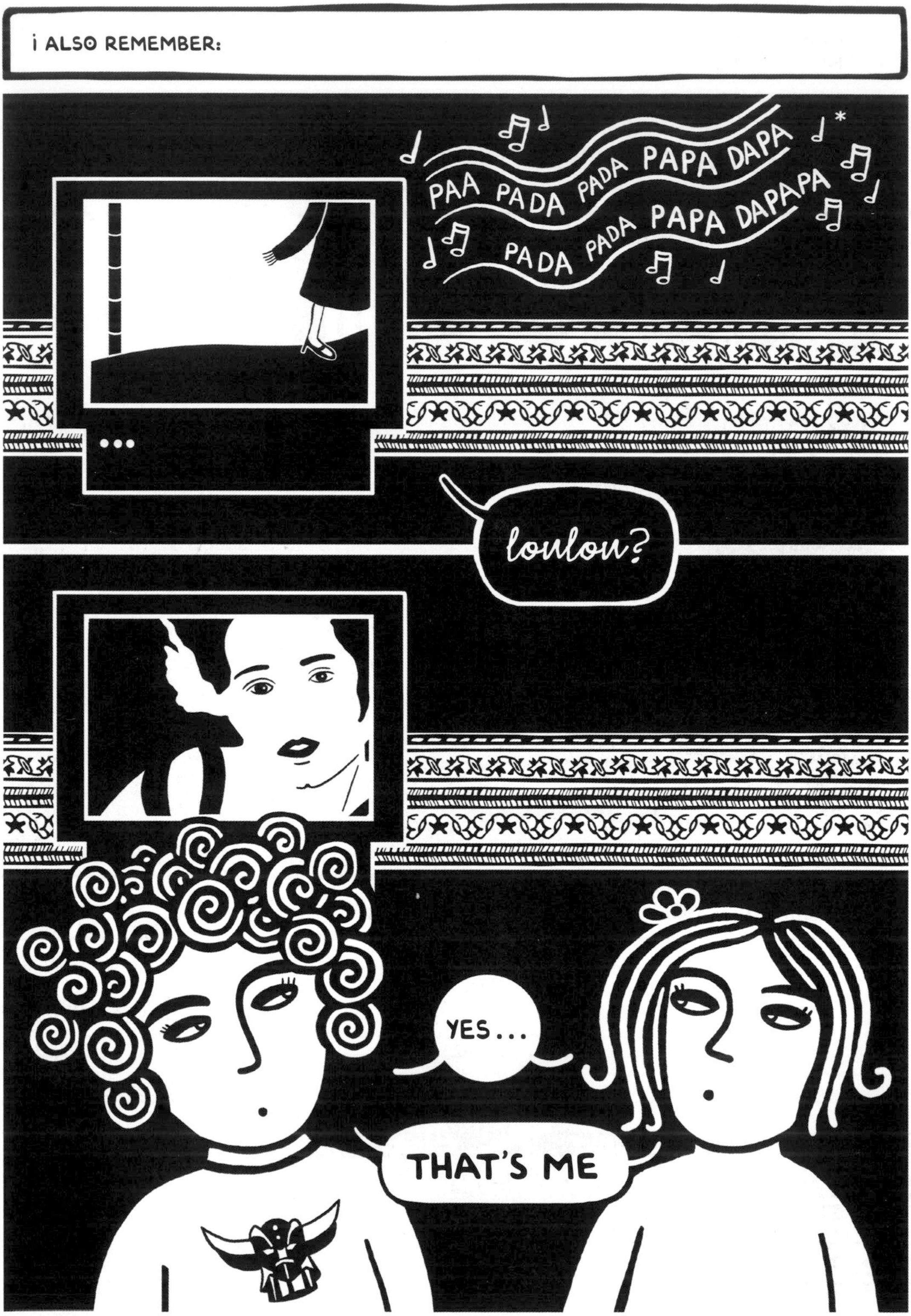
I ALSO REMEMBER:
PAA PADA PADA PAPA DAPA *
PADA PADA PAPA DAPAPA
...
loulou?
YES...
THAT'S ME

* GABRIEL FAURÉ'S PAVANE IN F-SHARP MINOR

I REMEMBER THAT DURING THE WAR, MY FATHER GOT INTO THE HABIT OF CRANKING UP THE VOLUME ON HIS MUSIC.

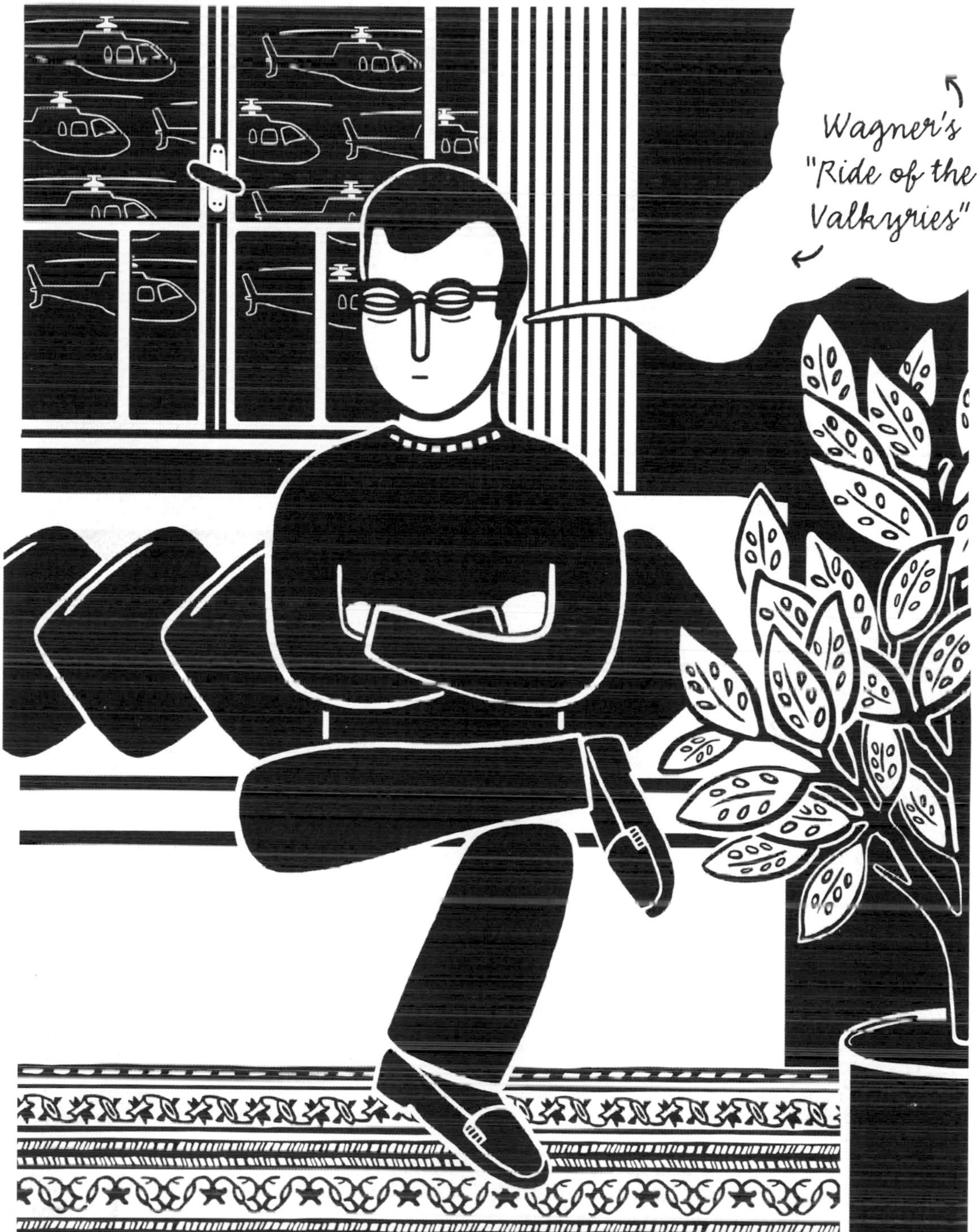
Wagner's "Ride of the Valkyries"

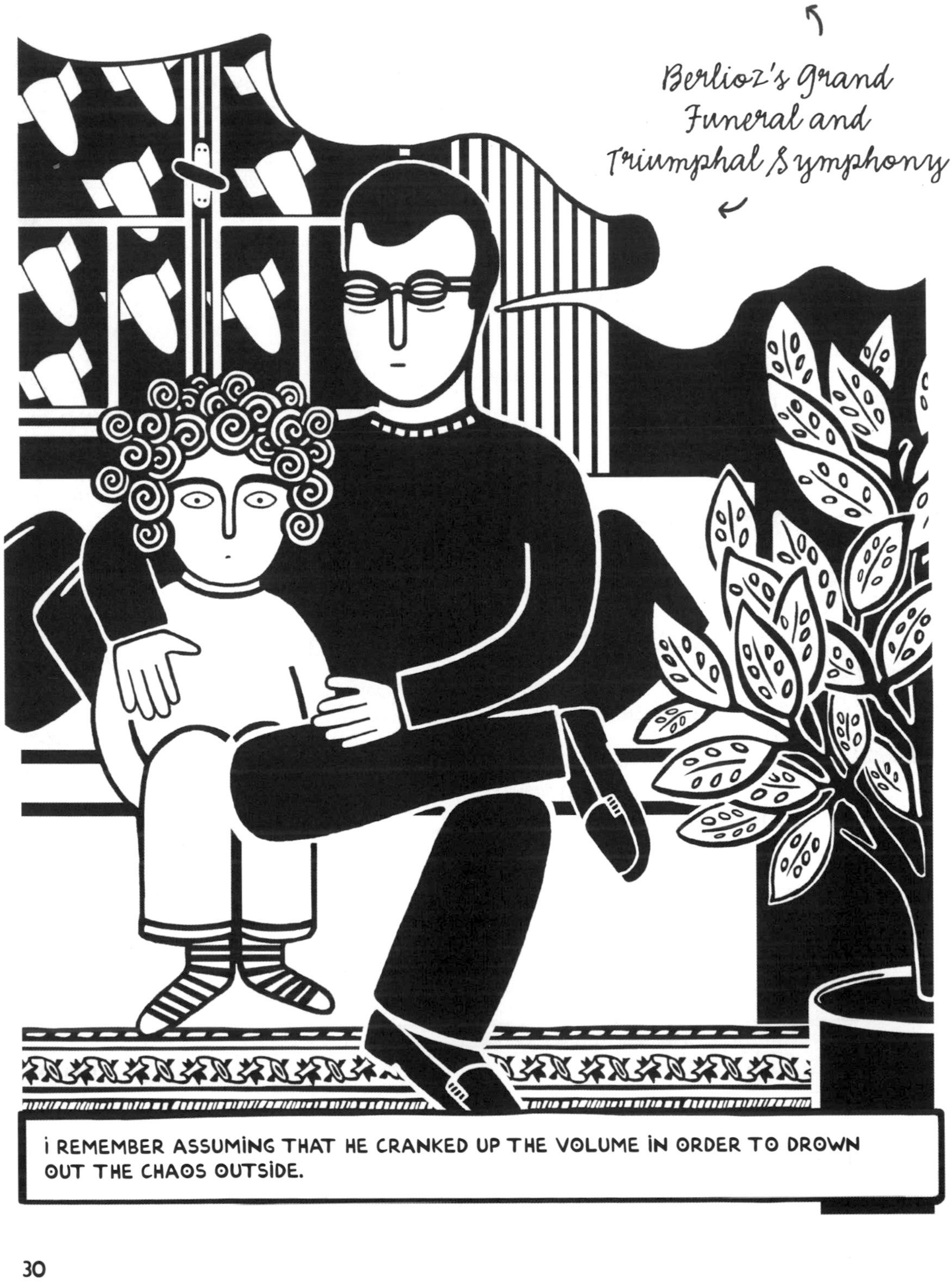
Berlioz's Grand Funeral and Triumphal Symphony
I REMEMBER ASSUMING THAT HE CRANKED UP THE VOLUME IN ORDER TO DROWN OUT THE CHAOS OUTSIDE.

BUT WHEN THE WAR GREW QUIET, HE KEPT CRANKING THE VOLUME UP.

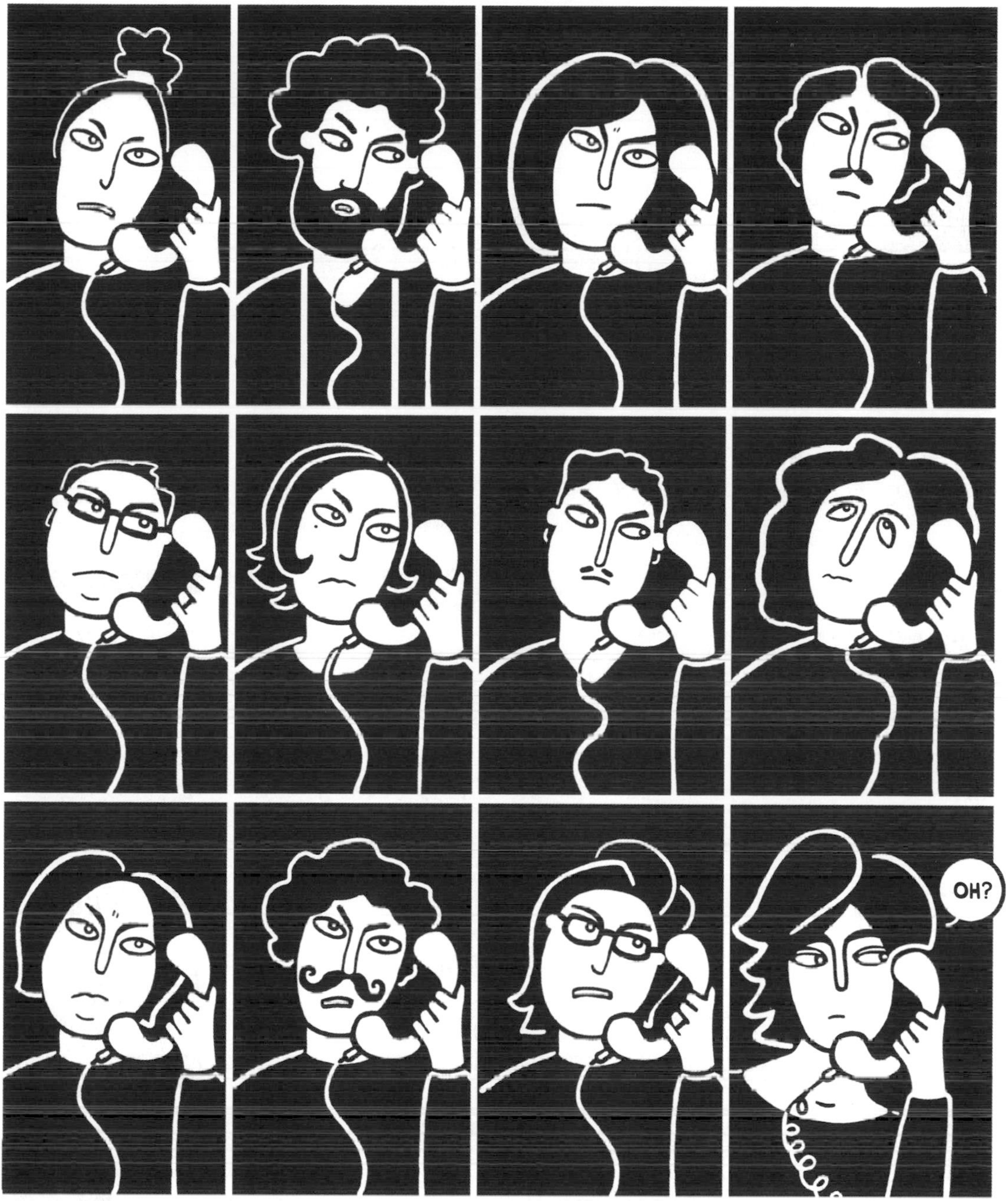
OH?

AND I REMEMBER THAT THE NEIGHBORS BEGAN TO COMPLAIN.

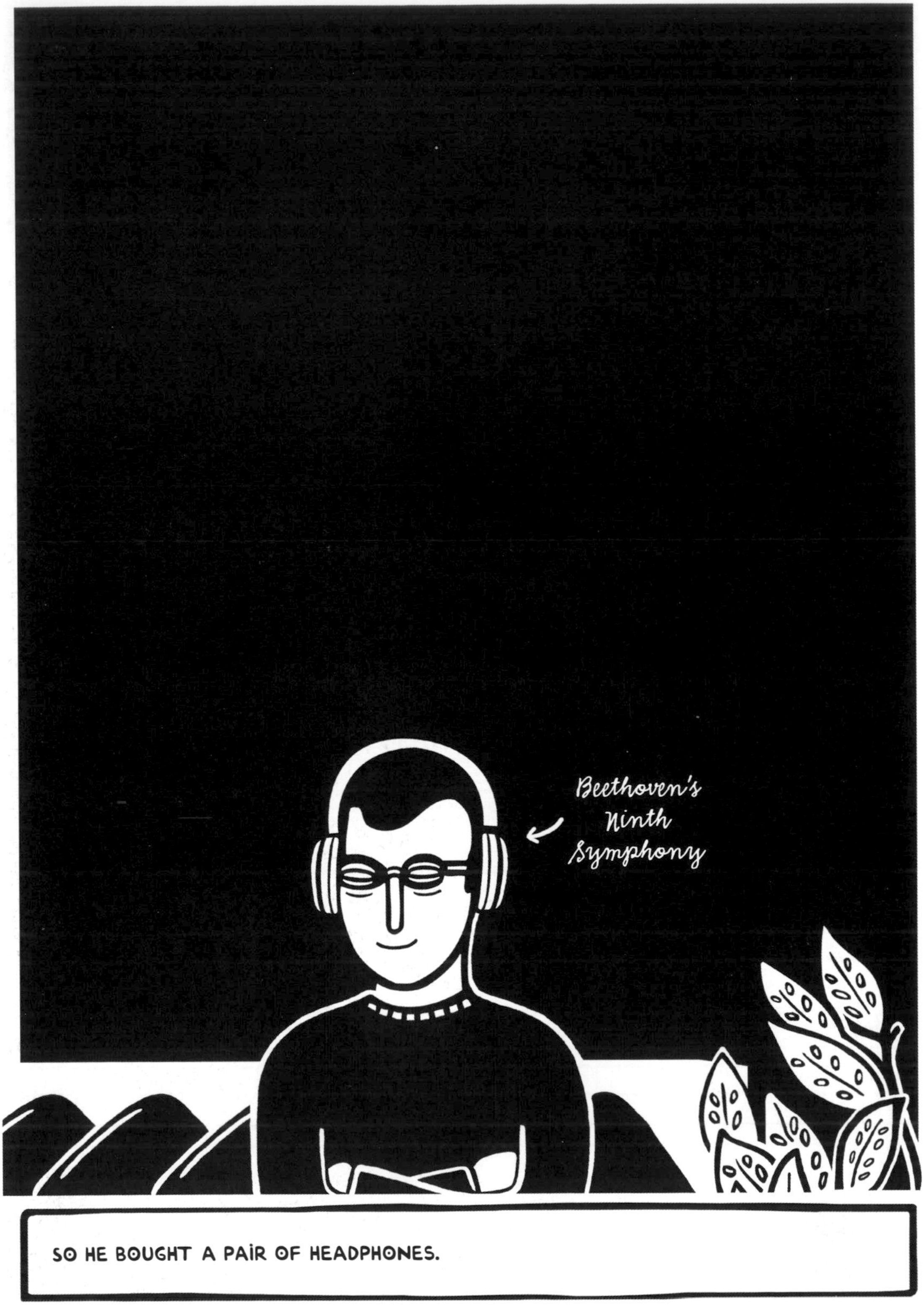
Beethoven's Ninth Symphony
SO HE BOUGHT A PAIR OF HEADPHONES.

I REMEMBER THE NIGHT OF JANUARY 27, 1989.

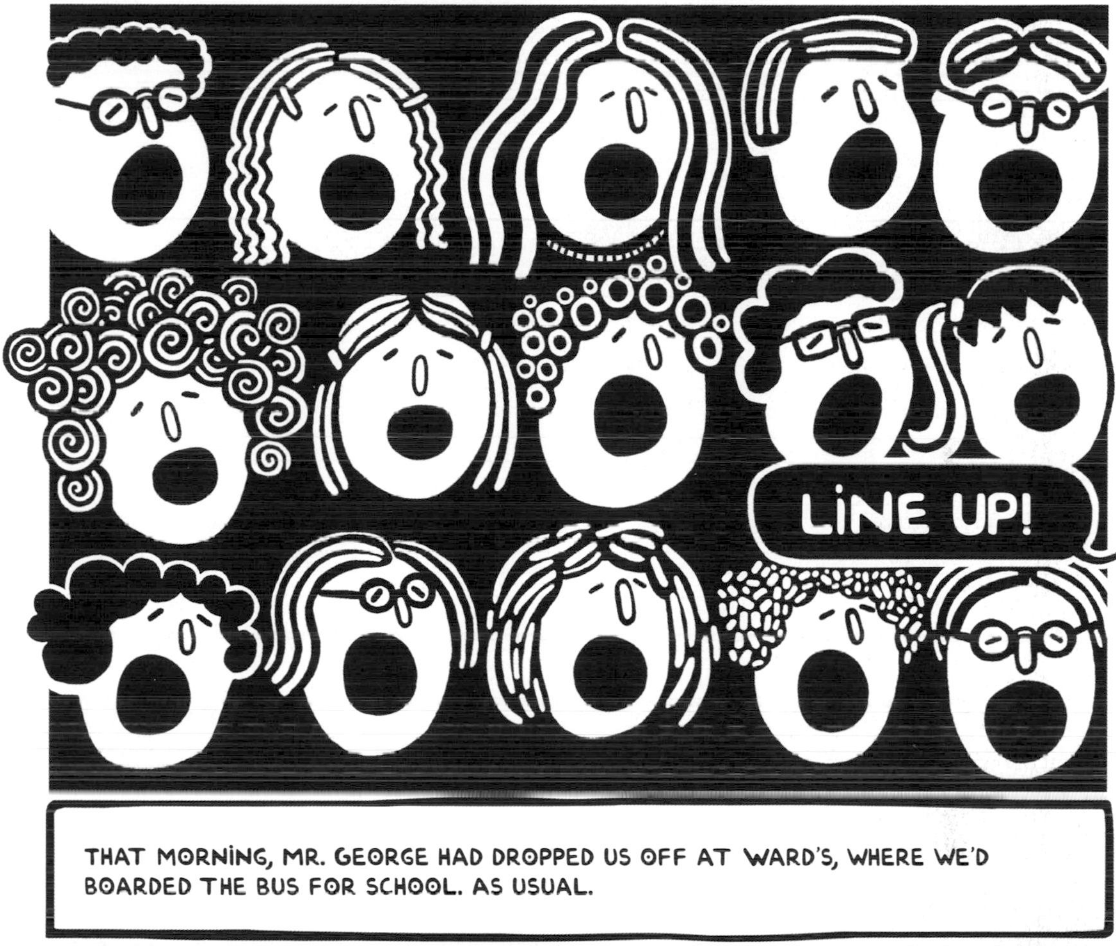
LINE UP!

THAT MORNING, MR. GEORGE HAD DROPPED US OFF AT WARD'S, WHERE WE'D BOARDED THE BUS FOR SCHOOL. AS USUAL.

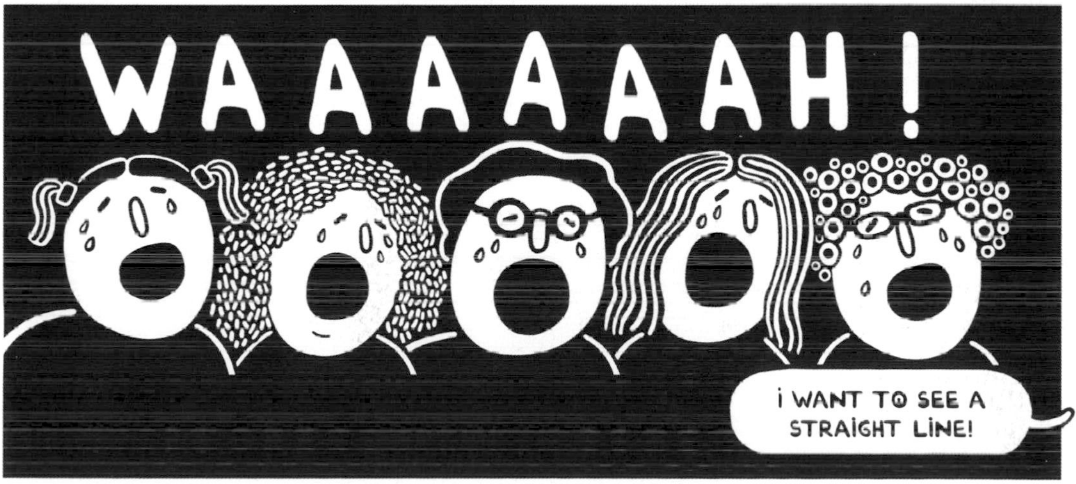
WAAAAAAH!
I WANT TO SEE A STRAIGHT LINE!

THAT DAY, SKIRMISHES HAD BROKEN OUT ON THE ROAD THAT LED TO SCHOOL.

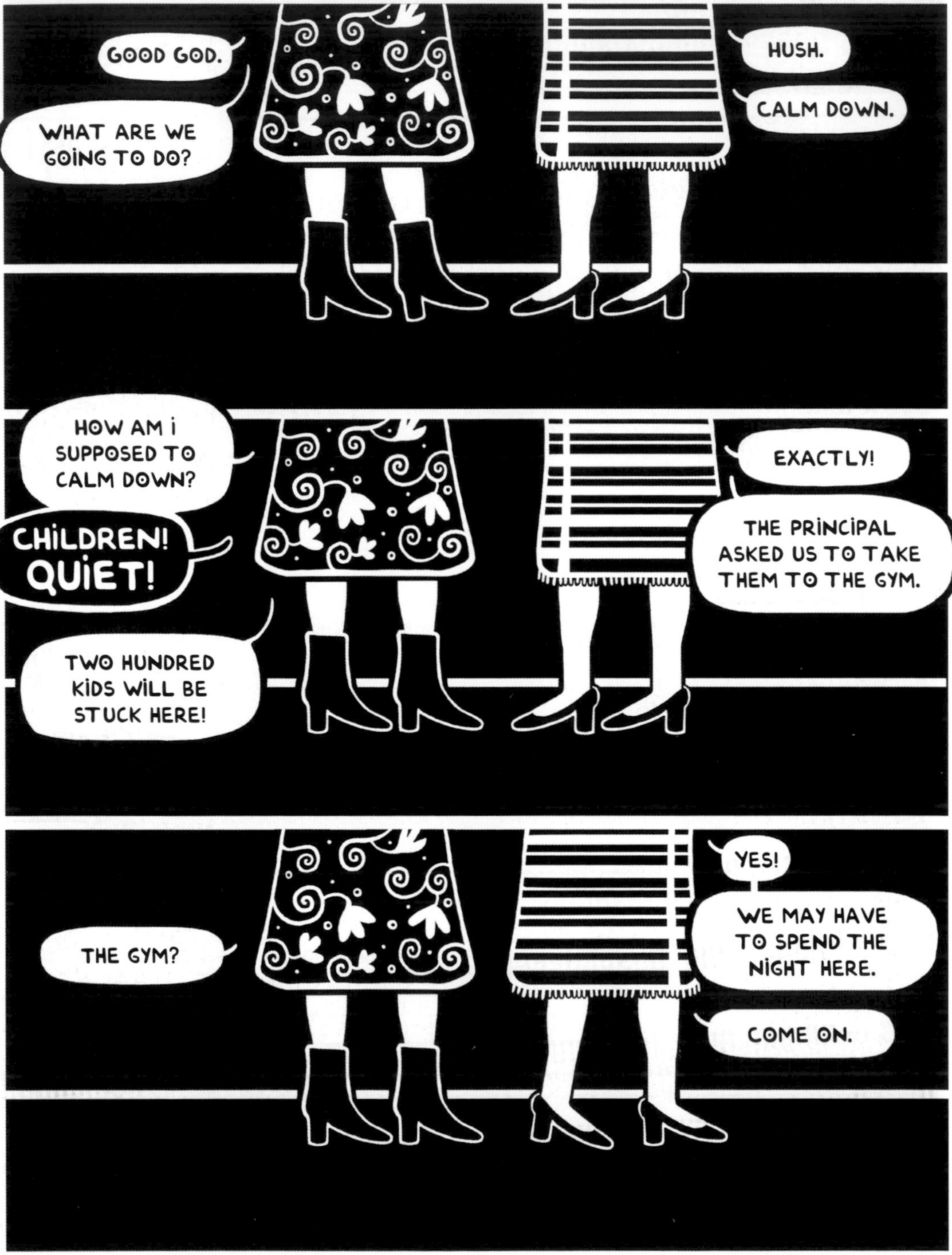
GOOD GOD.
WHAT ARE WE GOING TO DO?
HUSH.
CALM DOWN.
HOW AM I SUPPOSED TO CALM DOWN?
CHILDREN! QUIET!
TWO HUNDRED KIDS WILL BE STUCK HERE!
EXACTLY!
THE PRINCIPAL ASKED US TO TAKE THEM TO THE GYM.
THE GYM?
YES!
WE MAY HAVE TO SPEND THE NIGHT HERE.
COME ON.

ONCE WE WERE IN THE GYM, OUR TEACHERS PASSED OUT WATER AND CHEESE SANDWICHES.

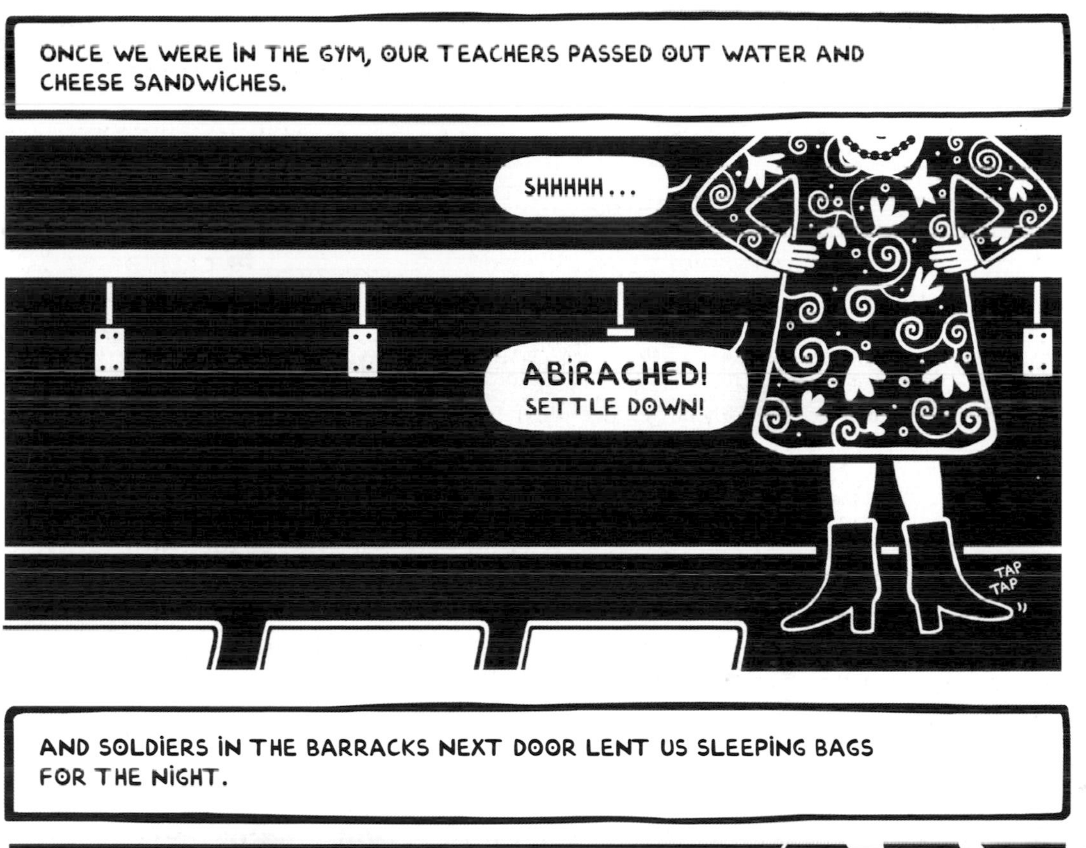

SHHHHH...
ABIRACHED! SETTLE DOWN!
TAP TAP

AND SOLDIERS IN THE BARRACKS NEXT DOOR LENT US SLEEPING BAGS FOR THE NIGHT.

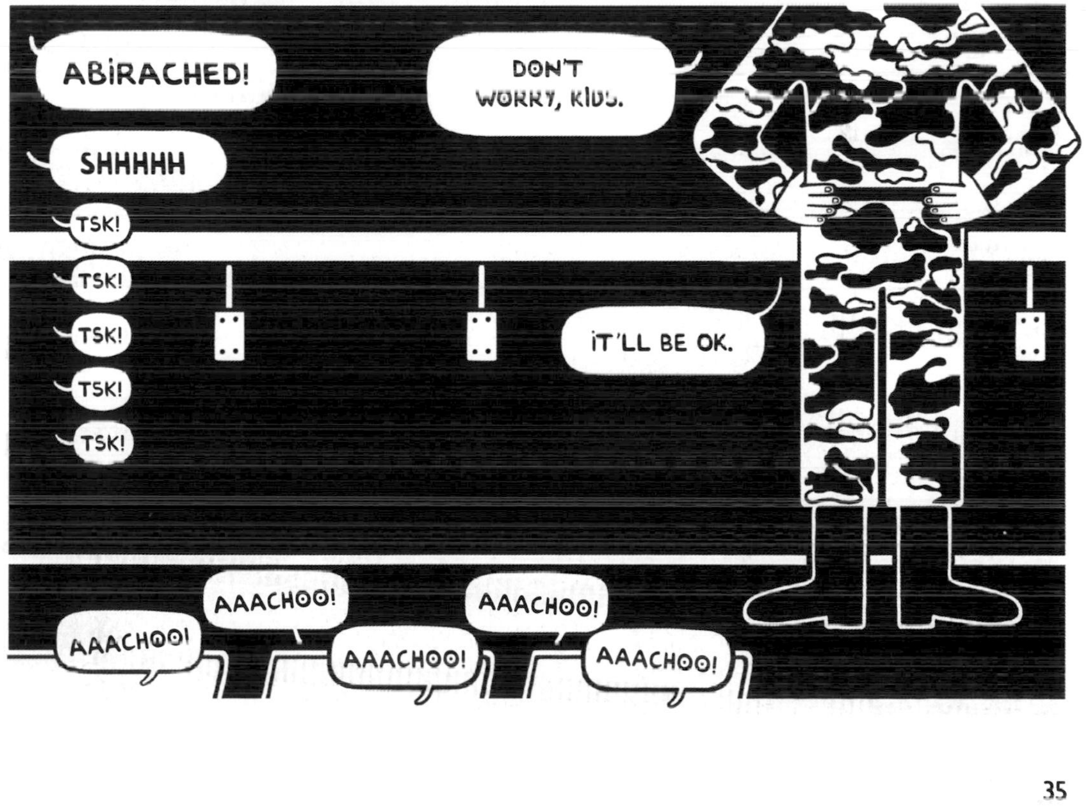

ABIRACHED!
SHHHHH
TSK!
TSK!
TSK!
TSK!
TSK!
DON'T WORRY, KIDS.
IT'LL BE OK.
AAACHOO!
AAACHOO!
AAACHOO!
AAACHOO!
AAACHOO!

I REMEMBER REALIZING OUR TEACHERS WERE AS SCARED AS WE WERE.

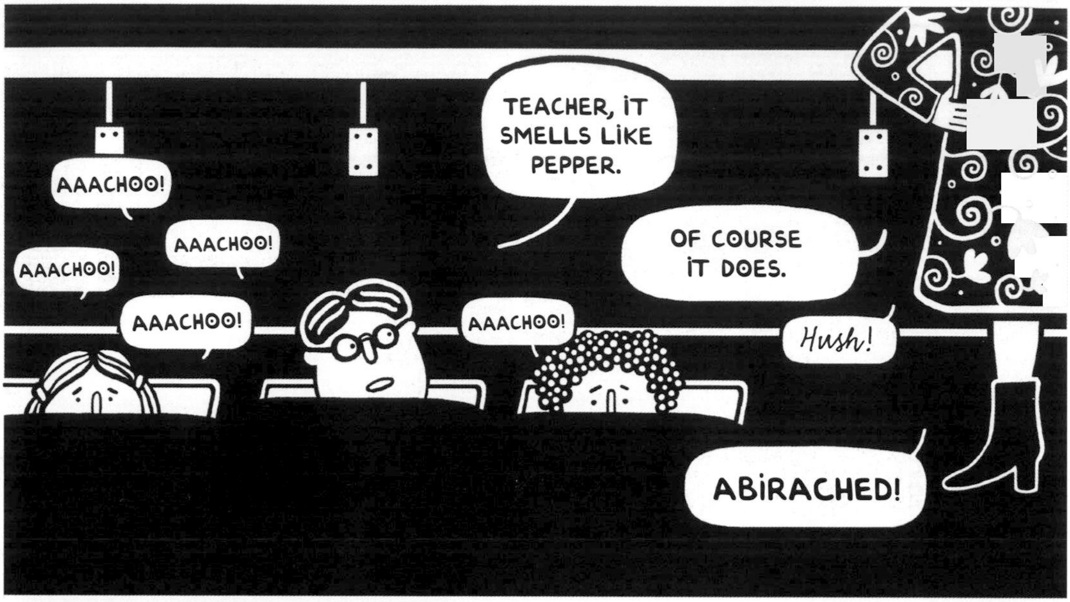

AAACHOO!
AAACHOO!
AAACHOO!
AAACHOO!
TEACHER, IT SMELLS LIKE PEPPER.
AAACHOO!
OF COURSE IT DOES.
Hush!
ABIRACHED!

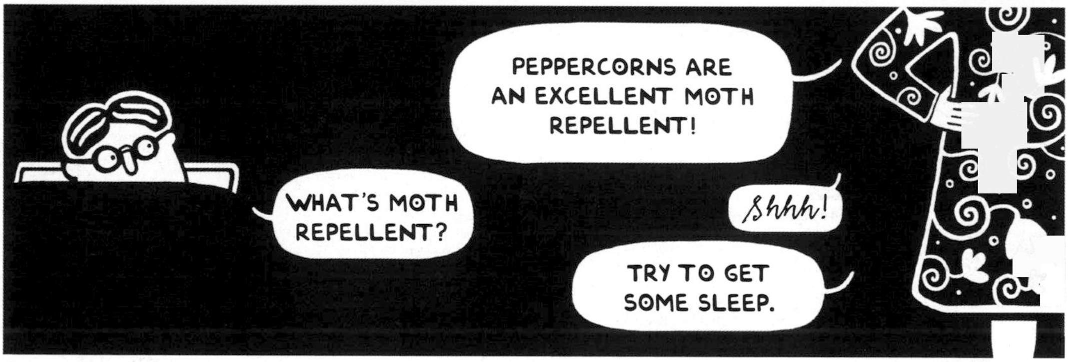

PEPPERCORNS ARE AN EXCELLENT MOTH REPELLENT!
WHAT'S MOTH REPELLENT?
Shhh!
TRY TO GET SOME SLEEP.

I REMEMBER GLIMPSING, IN A CORNER OF THE GYM, THE TIPS OF THEIR CIGARETTES GLOWING IN THE DARK.

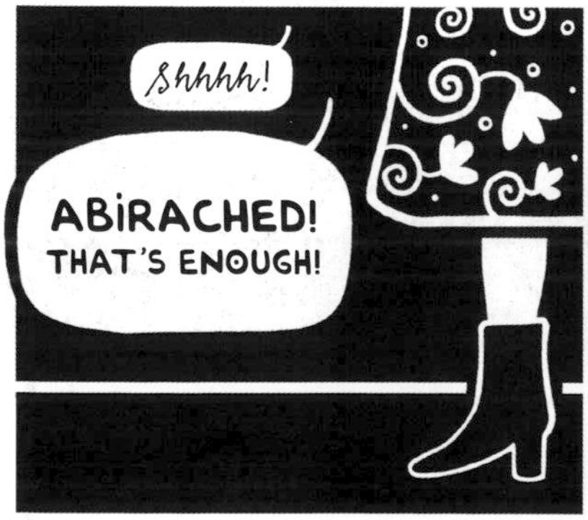

Shhhh!
ABIRACHED! THAT'S ENOUGH!

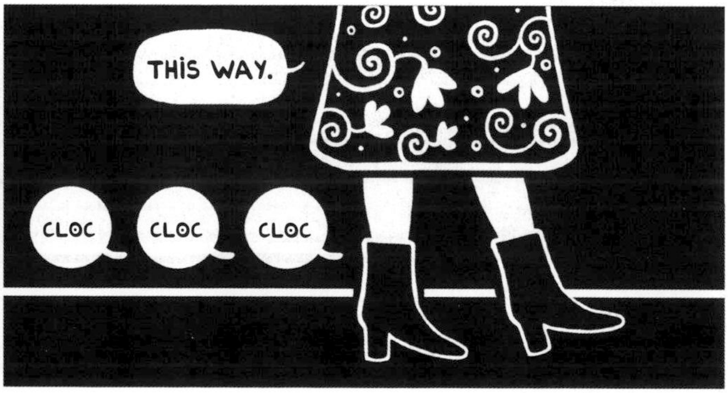

THIS WAY.
CLOC
CLOC
CLOC

I DON'T REMEMBER WHAT HAPPENED NEXT, SINCE I FINALLY GOT PUNISHED. I SPENT THE REST OF THE NIGHT LOCKED UP IN THE GYM BATHROOM.

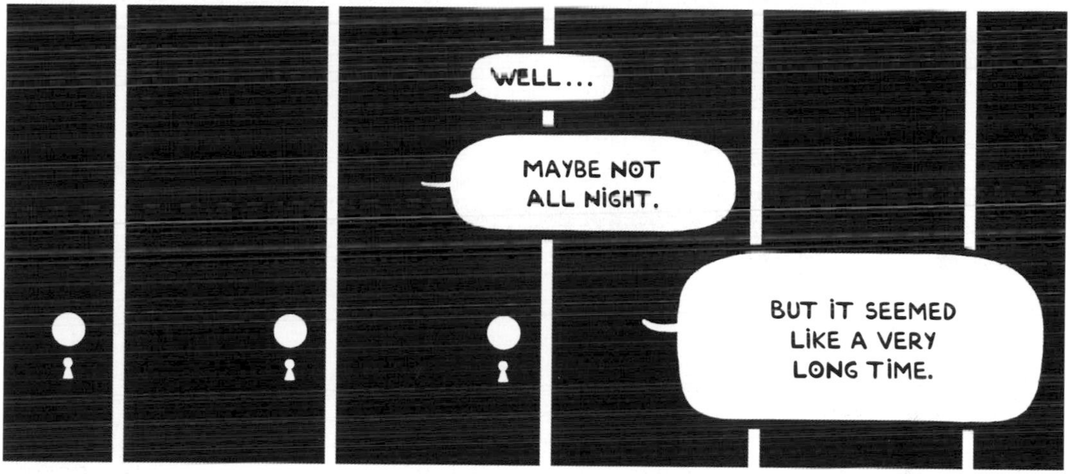
WELL...
MAYBE NOT ALL NIGHT.
BUT IT SEEMED LIKE A VERY LONG TIME.

THE NEXT MORNING, MY MOTHER AND CHUCRI CAME TO GET US IN THE R12.

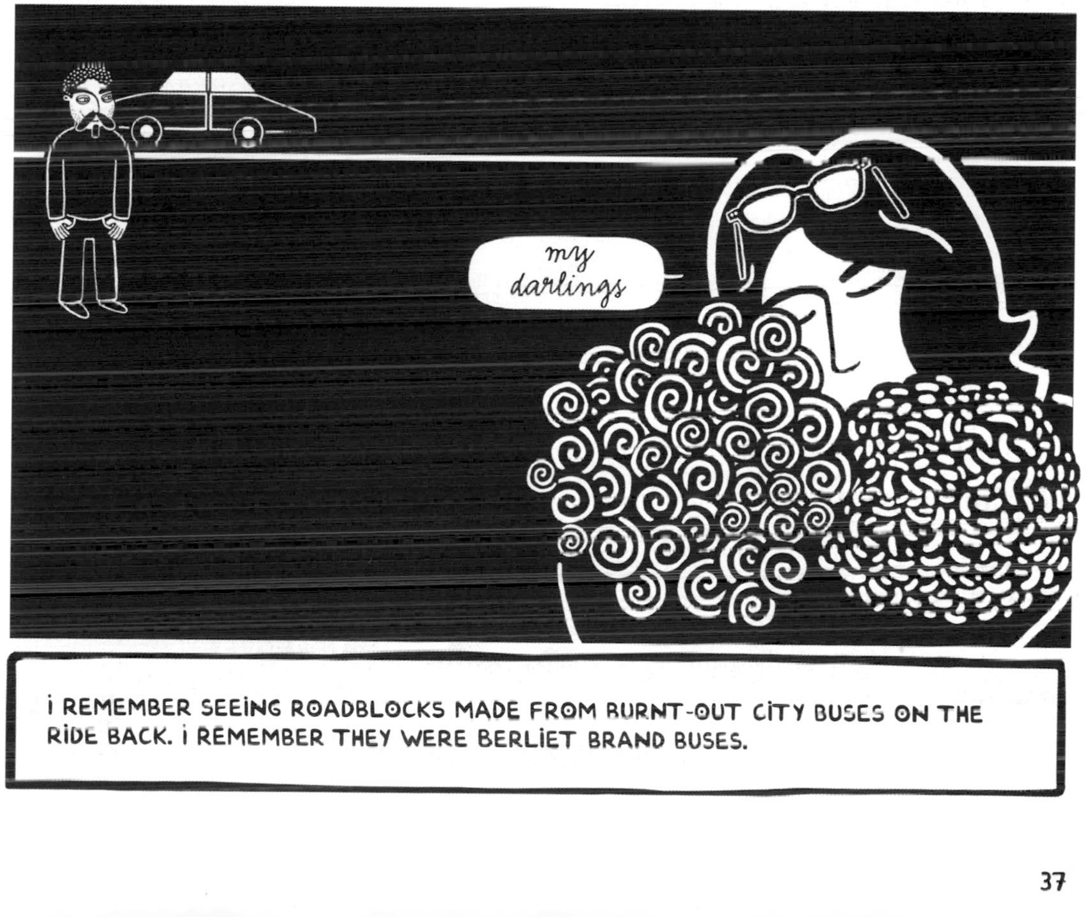
my darlings

I REMEMBER SEEING ROADBLOCKS MADE FROM BURNT-OUT CITY BUSES ON THE RIDE BACK. I REMEMBER THEY WERE BERLIET BRAND BUSES.

TWO DAYS LATER, WE CELEBRATED MY MOTHER'S BIRTHDAY.
ANHALA MADE A CHOCOLATE CAKE.

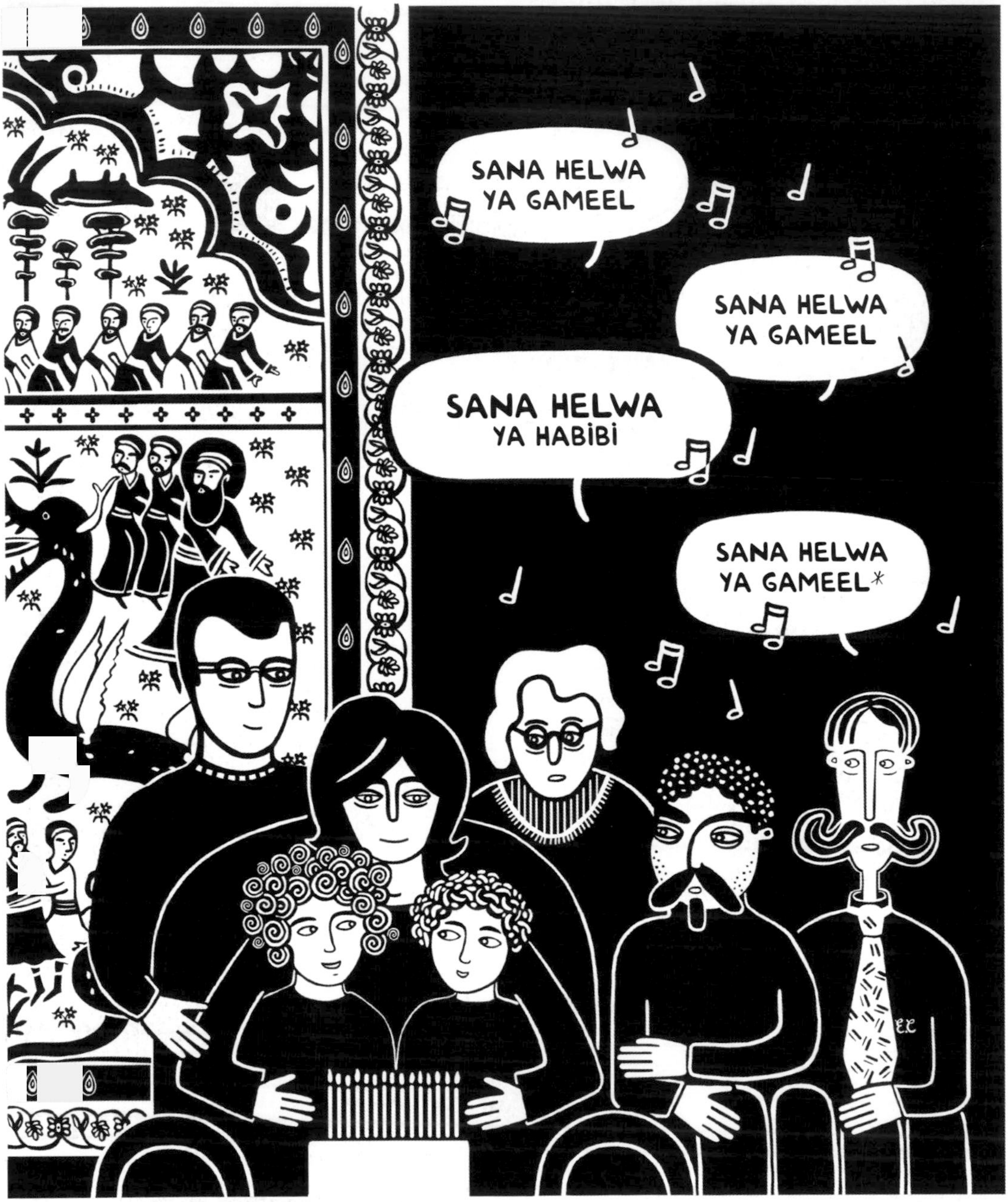
SANA HELWA
YA GAMEEL
SANA HELWA
YA GAMEEL
SANA HELWA
YA HABIBI
SANA HELWA
YA GAMEEL*

AS FOR US: WE WERE ON VACATION.

* A POPULAR BIRTHDAY SONG

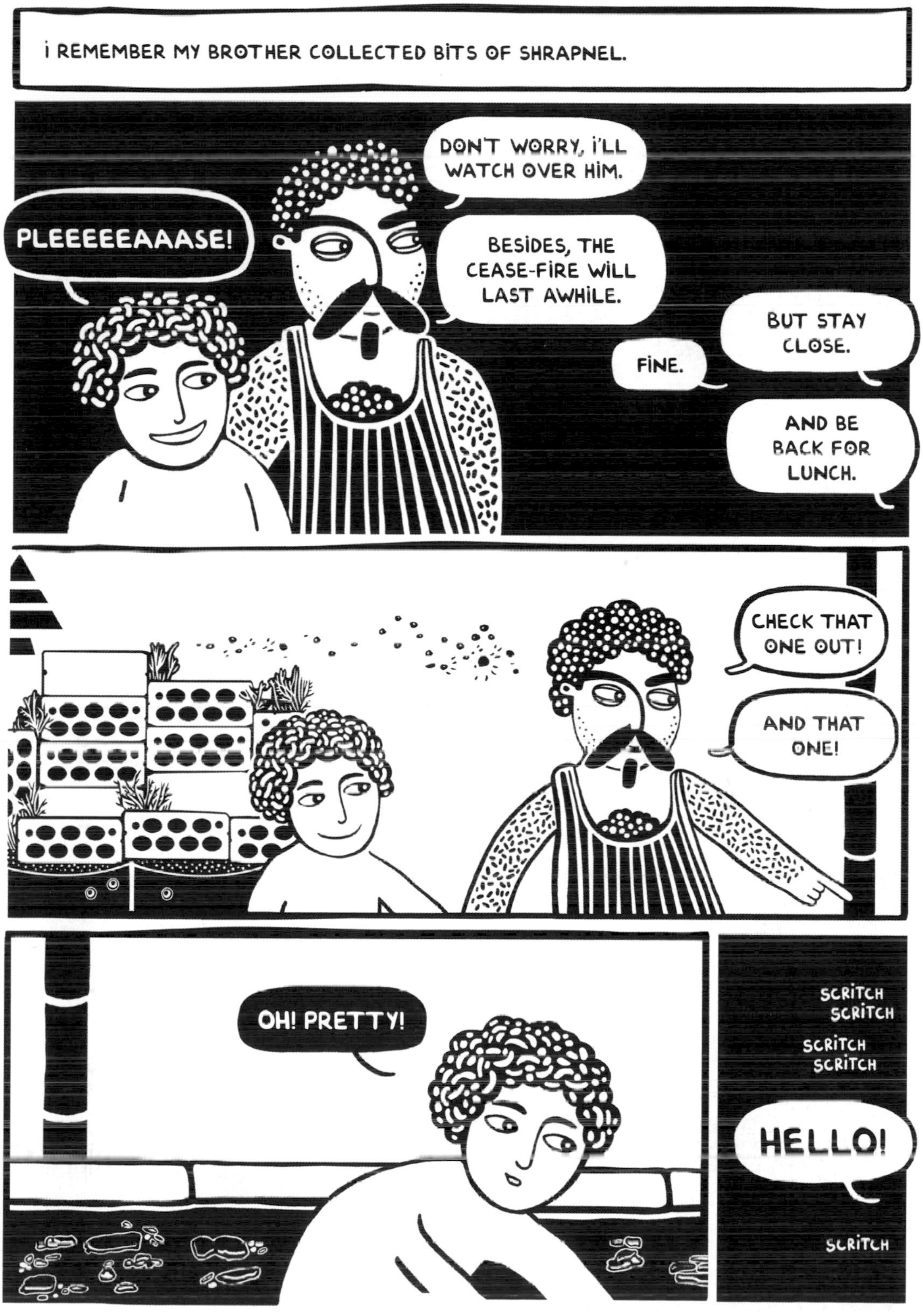
I REMEMBER MY BROTHER COLLECTED BITS OF SHRAPNEL.
PLEEEEEEAAASE!
DON'T WORRY, I'LL WATCH OVER HIM.
BESIDES, THE CEASE-FIRE WILL LAST AWHILE.
FINE.
BUT STAY CLOSE.
AND BE BACK FOR LUNCH.
CHECK THAT ONE OUT!
AND THAT ONE!
OH! PRETTY!
SCRITCH SCRITCH
SCRITCH SCRITCH
HELLO!
SCRITCH

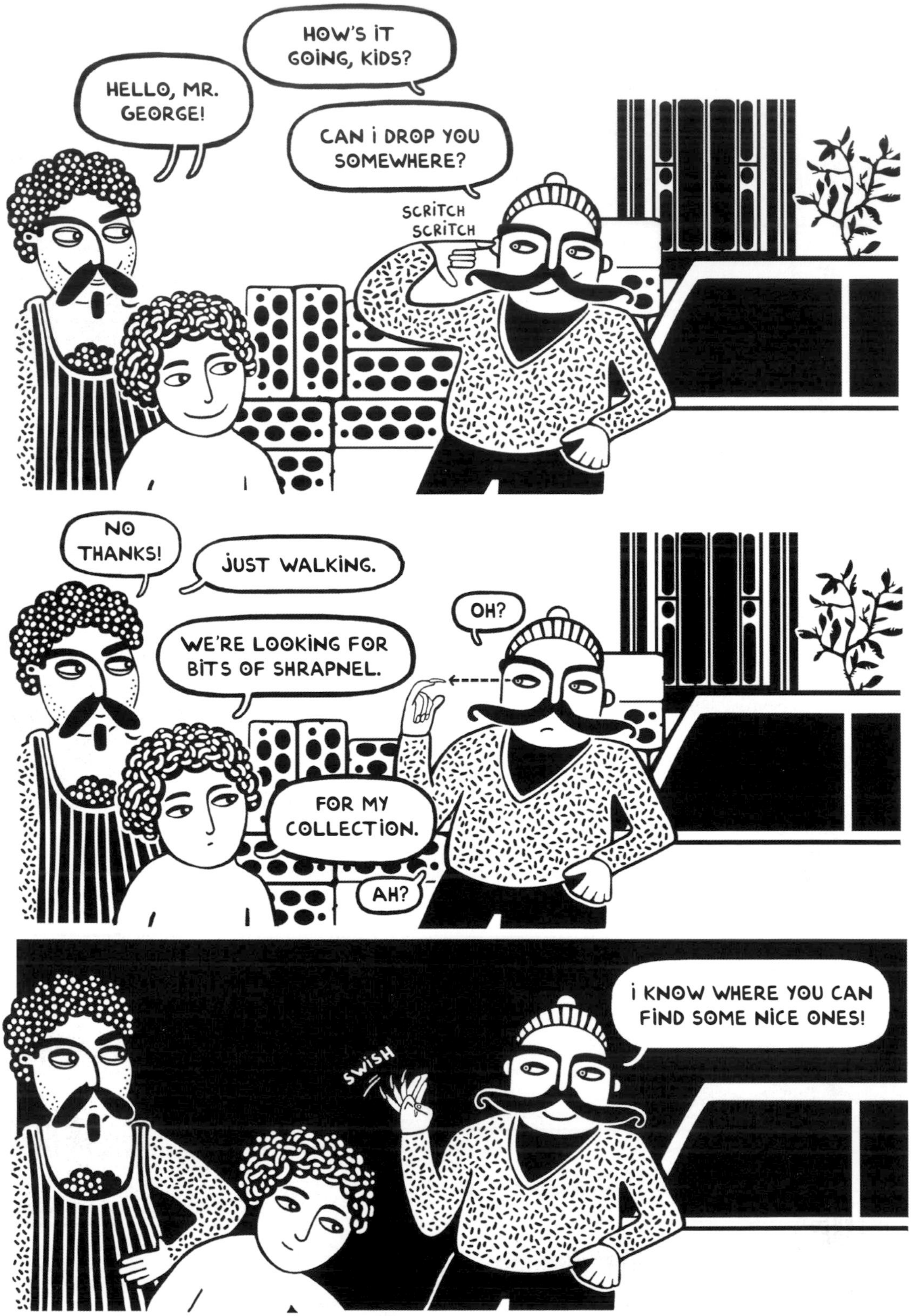
HELLO, MR. GEORGE!
HOW'S IT GOING, KIDS?
CAN I DROP YOU SOMEWHERE?
SCRITCH SCRITCH
NO THANKS!
JUST WALKING.
WE'RE LOOKING FOR BITS OF SHRAPNEL.
OH?
FOR MY COLLECTION.
AH?
SWISH
I KNOW WHERE YOU CAN FIND SOME NICE ONES!

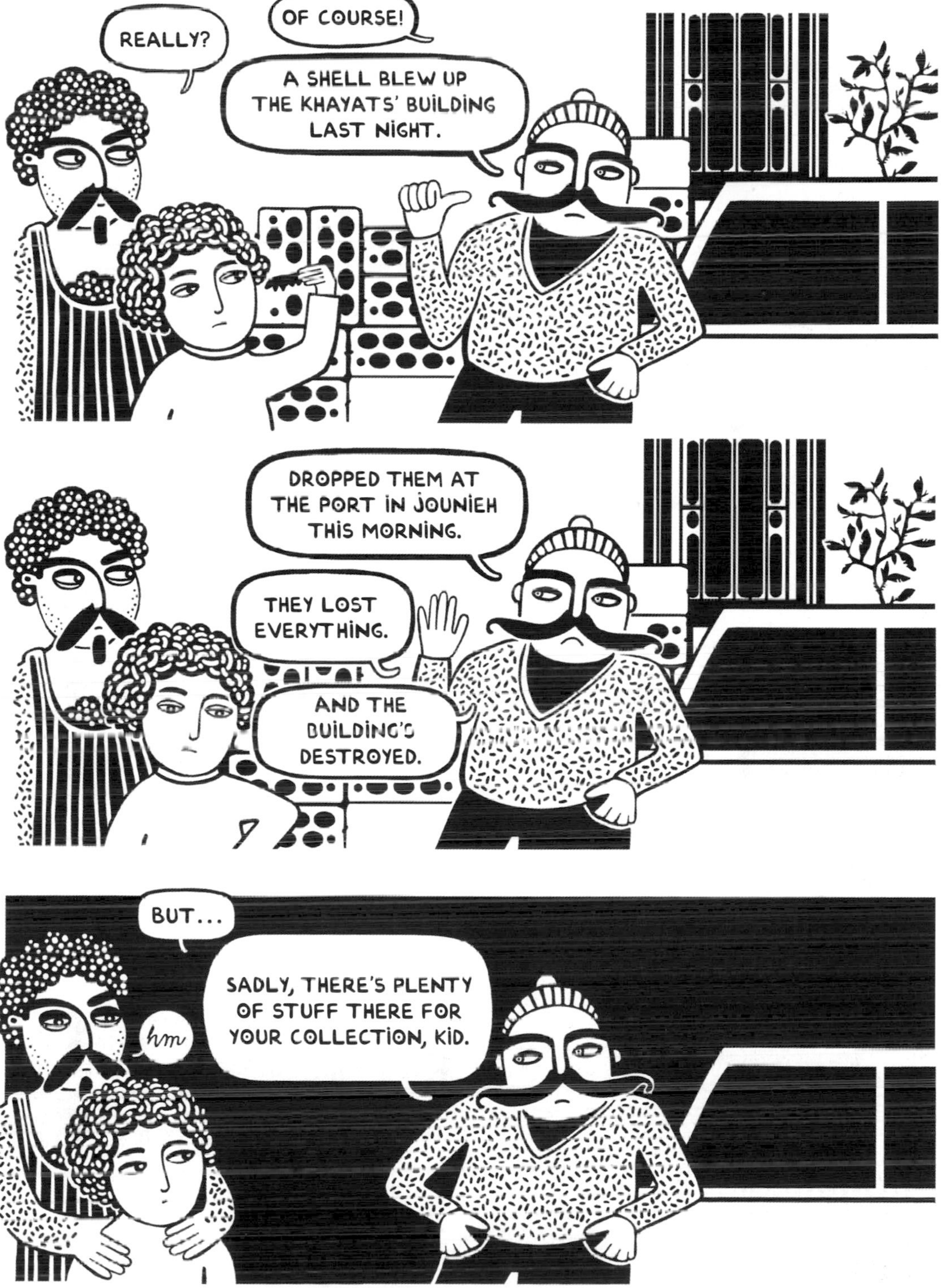
REALLY?
OF COURSE!
A SHELL BLEW UP THE KHAYATS' BUILDING LAST NIGHT.
DROPPED THEM AT THE PORT IN JOUNIEH THIS MORNING.
THEY LOST EVERYTHING.
AND THE BUILDING'S DESTROYED.
BUT...
hm
SADLY, THERE'S PLENTY OF STUFF THERE FOR YOUR COLLECTION, KID.

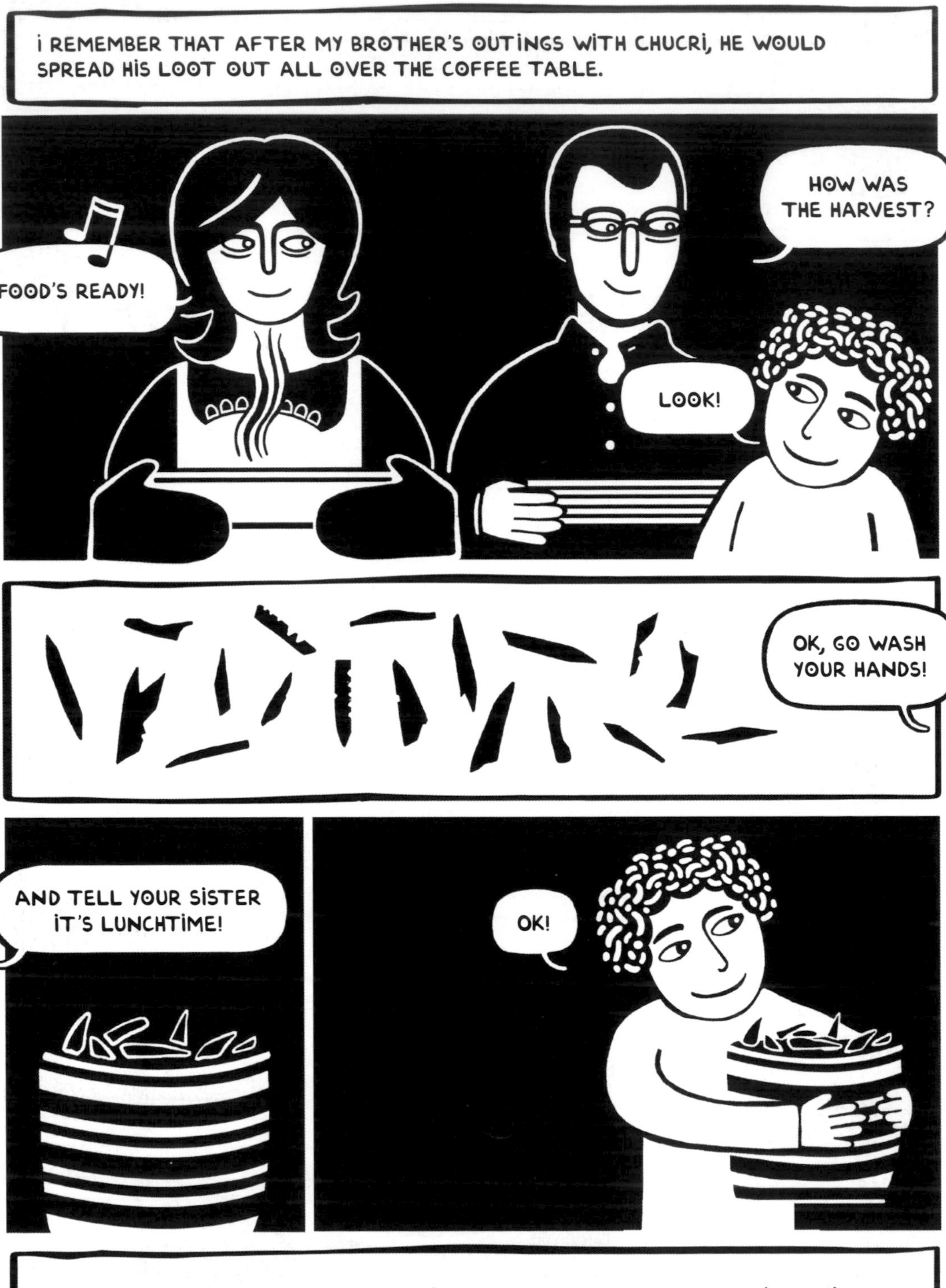
I REMEMBER THAT AFTER MY BROTHER'S OUTINGS WITH CHUCRI, HE WOULD SPREAD HIS LOOT OUT ALL OVER THE COFFEE TABLE.
FOOD'S READY!
HOW WAS THE HARVEST?
LOOK!
OK, GO WASH YOUR HANDS!
AND TELL YOUR SISTER IT'S LUNCHTIME!
OK!
THEN HE'D PUT THE SHRAPNEL AWAY IN A BASKET MY MOTHER HAD GIVEN HIM.

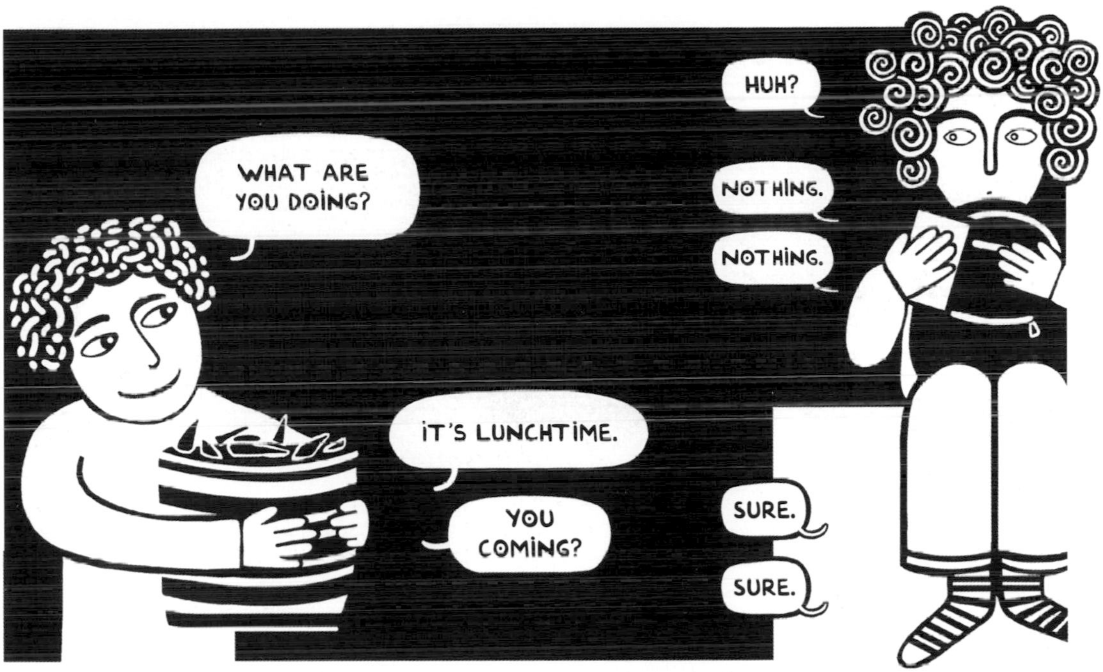
WHAT ARE YOU DOING?
HUH?
NOTHING.
NOTHING.
IT'S LUNCHTIME.
YOU COMING?
SURE.
SURE.

I REMEMBER THAT I HAD TAKEN TO LEAVING MY BACKPACK BY MY BED AT NIGHT.

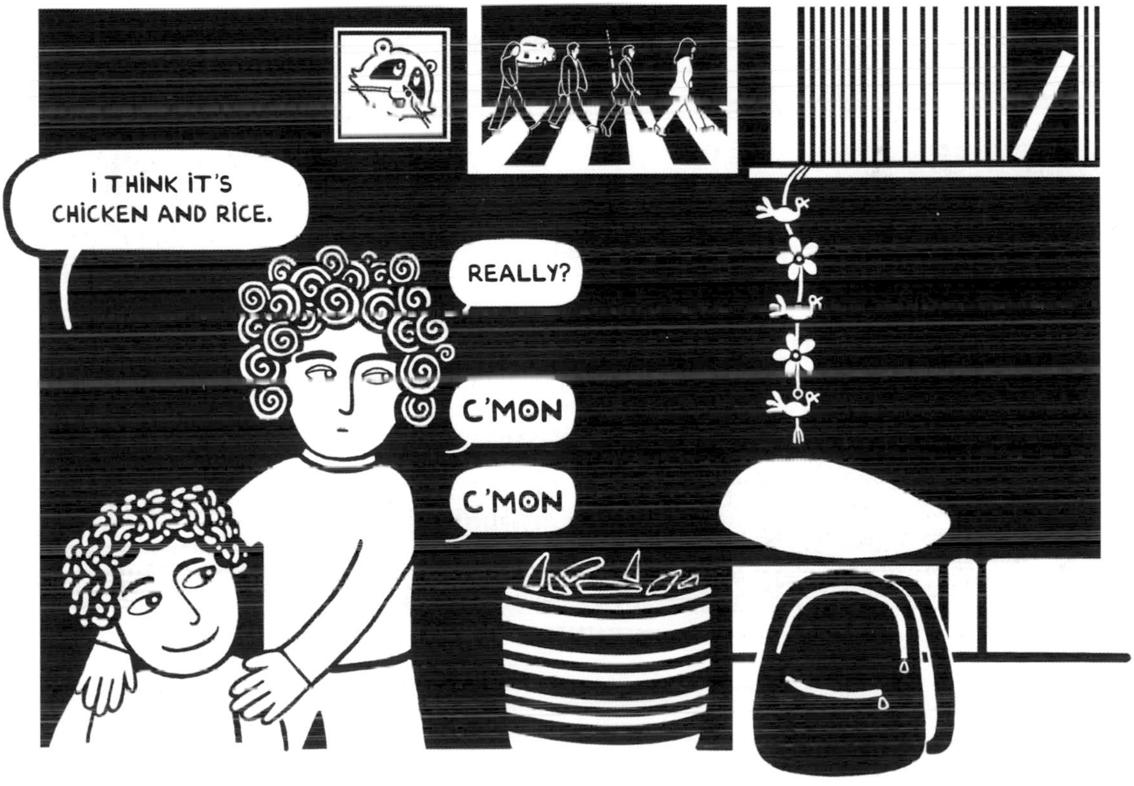
I THINK IT'S CHICKEN AND RICE.
REALLY?
C'MON
C'MON

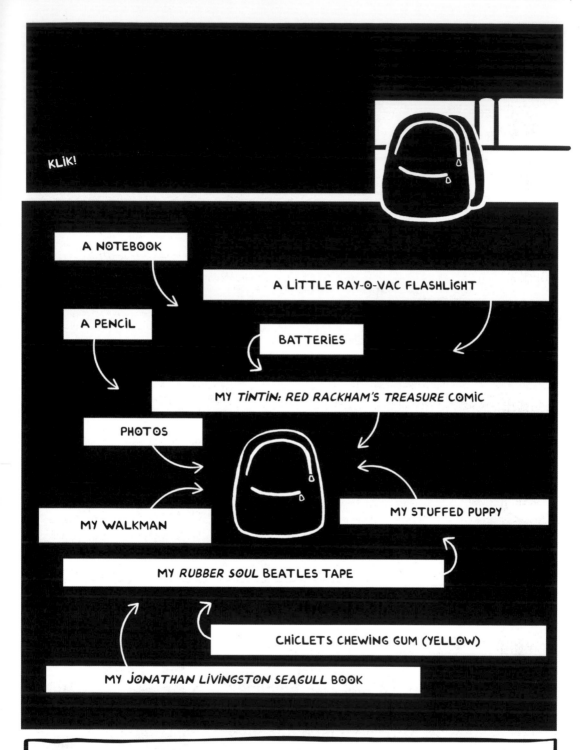

KLIK!

A NOTEBOOK

A LITTLE RAY-O-VAC FLASHLIGHT

A PENCIL

BATTERIES

MY *TINTIN: RED RACKHAM'S TREASURE* COMIC

PHOTOS

MY STUFFED PUPPY

MY WALKMAN

MY *RUBBER SOUL* BEATLES TAPE

CHICLETS CHEWING GUM (YELLOW)

MY *JONATHAN LIVINGSTON SEAGULL* BOOK

IN MY BACKPACK, I HAD EVERYTHING I WANTED TO TAKE WITH ME, IF WE HAD TO RUN.

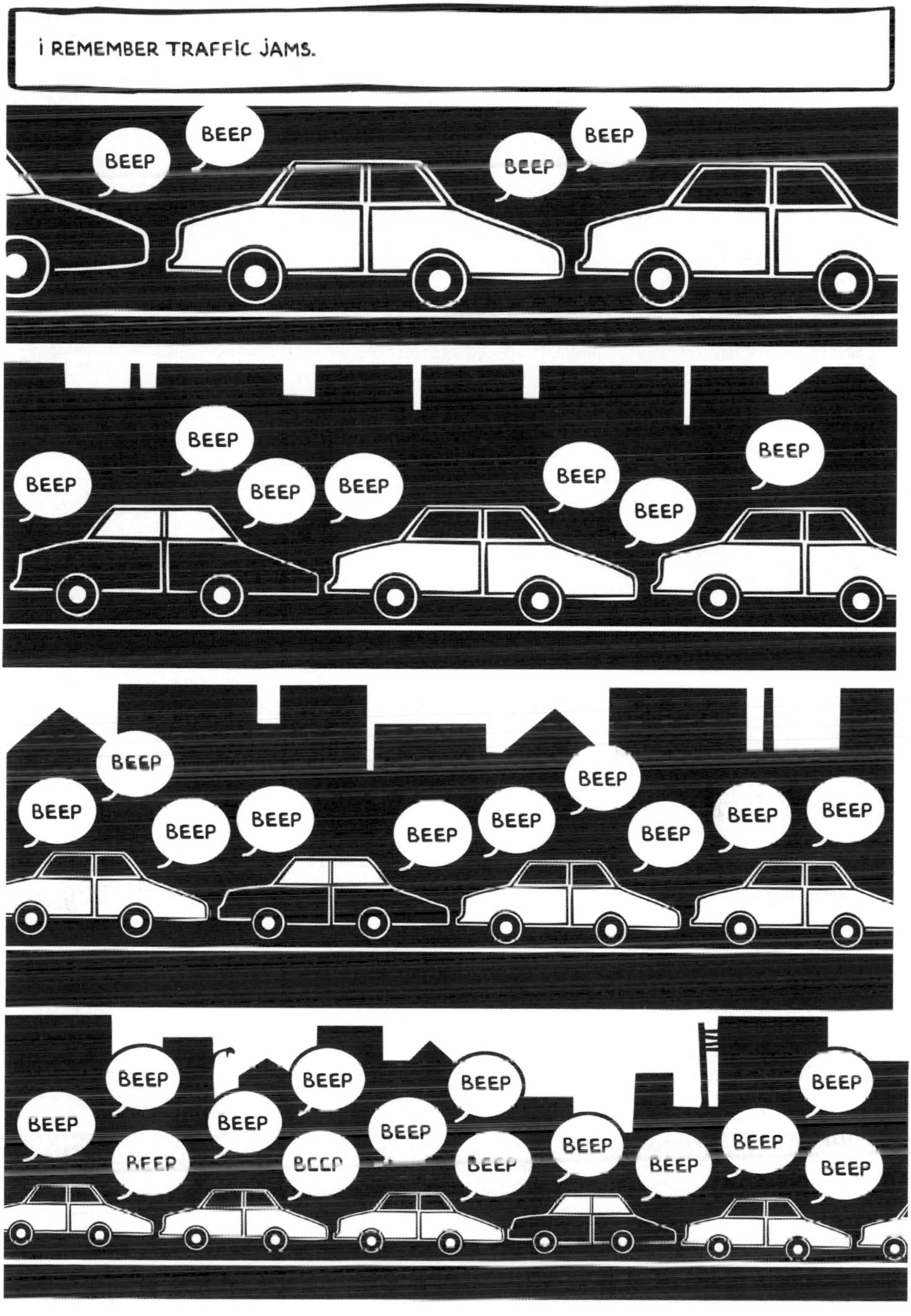
I REMEMBER TRAFFIC JAMS.
BEEP
BEEP
BEEP
BEEP
BEEP
BEEP
BEEP
BEEP
BEEP
BEEP
BEEP
BEEP
BEEP
BEEP
BEEP
BEEP
BEEP
BEEP
BEEP
BEEP
BEEP
BEEP
BEEP
BEEP
BEEP
BEEP
BEEP
BEEP
BEEP
BEEP
BEEP
BEEP
BEEP
BEEP
BEEP
BEEP
BEEP
BEEP
BEEP
BEEP

DURING THE WAR, MANY ROADS LINKING BEIRUT TO THE REST OF THE NATION WERE SHUT DOWN.

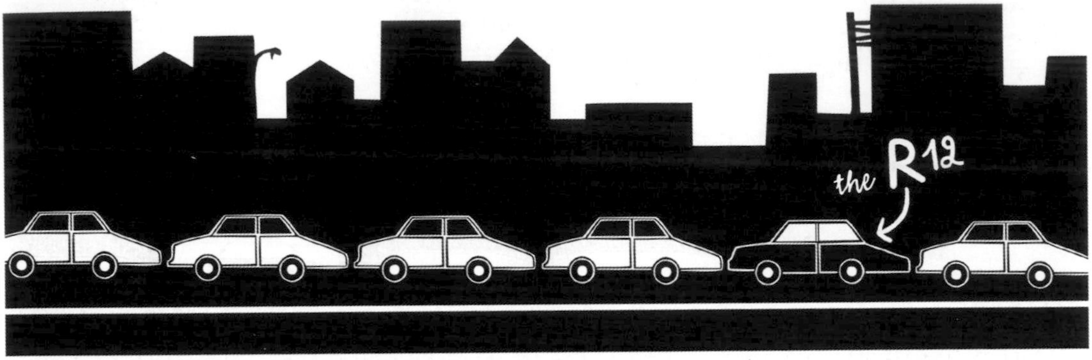
the R12

TRYING TO GET OUT OF THE CITY COULD TAKE FIVE HOURS...

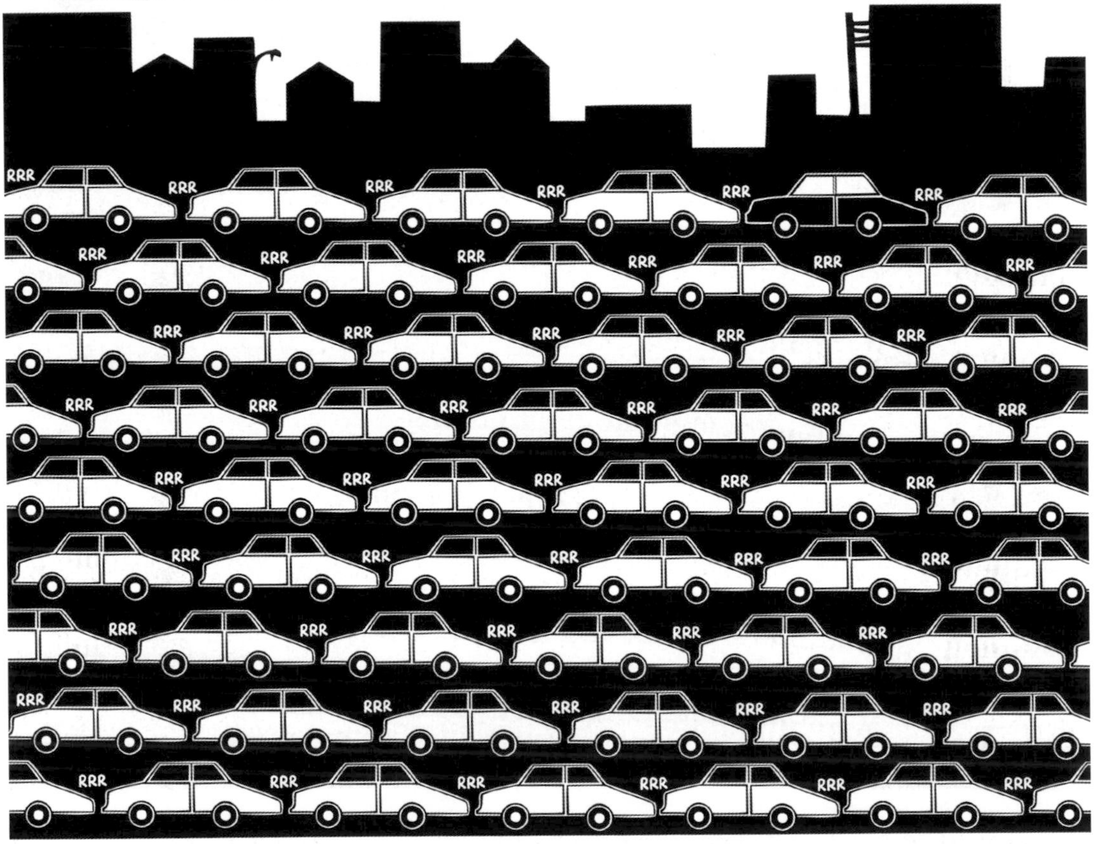
RRR
RRR
RRR
RRR
RRR
RRR

FOUR OF THEM AT A STANDSTILL.

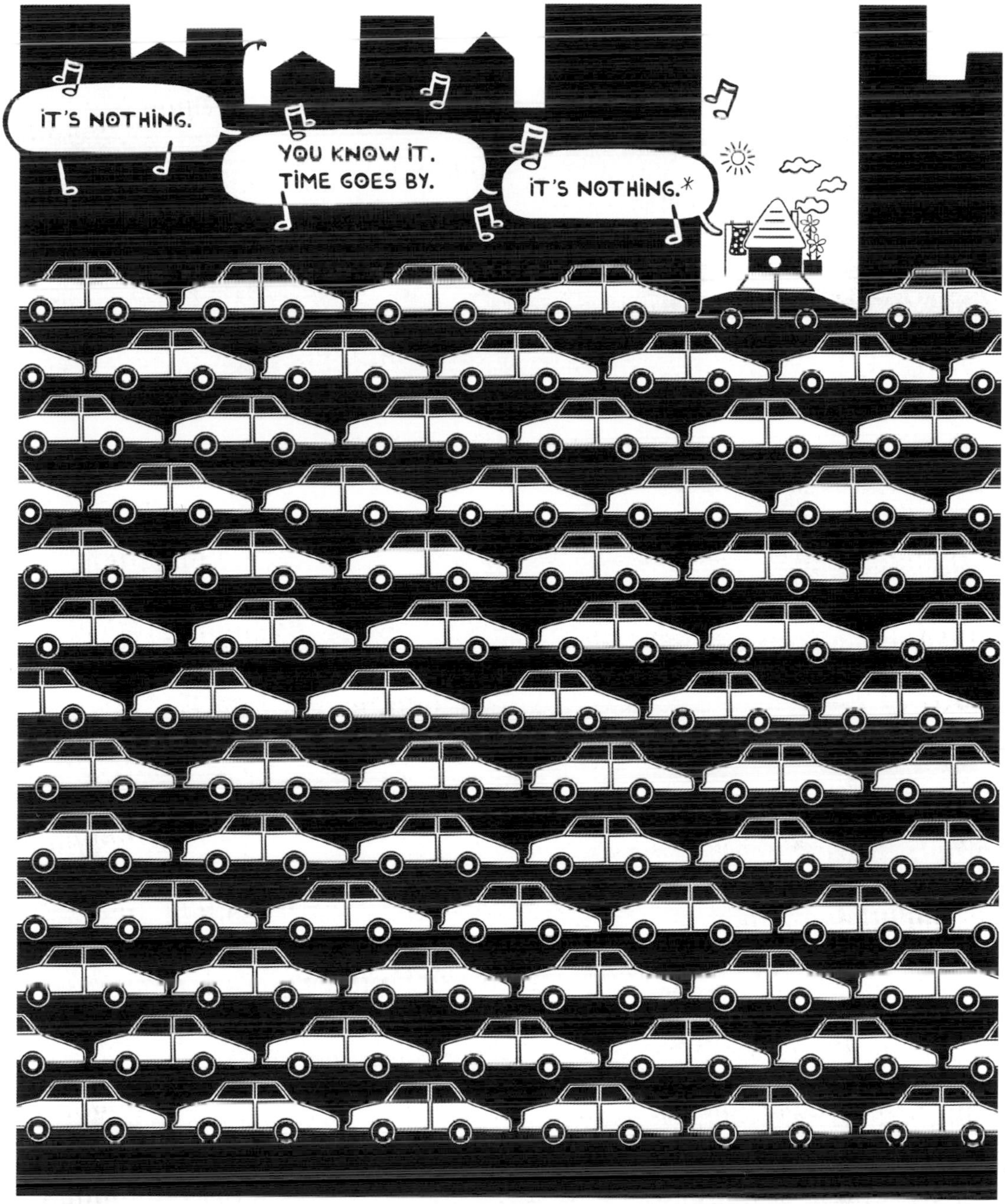
IT'S NOTHING.
YOU KNOW IT. TIME GOES BY.
IT'S NOTHING.*
I REMEMBER ALL THE THINGS MY MOTHER HAD IN THE CAR: WATER, FRUIT JUICE, SANDWICHES, CANDY, TISSUES, PILLOWS, BLANKETS, PLAYING CARDS, AND A BOOK OF RIDDLES...

* JULIEN CLERC, "CE N'EST RIEN," 1971

I REMEMBER ALL THE PLACES WHERE WE TOOK REFUGE DURING THE WAR.

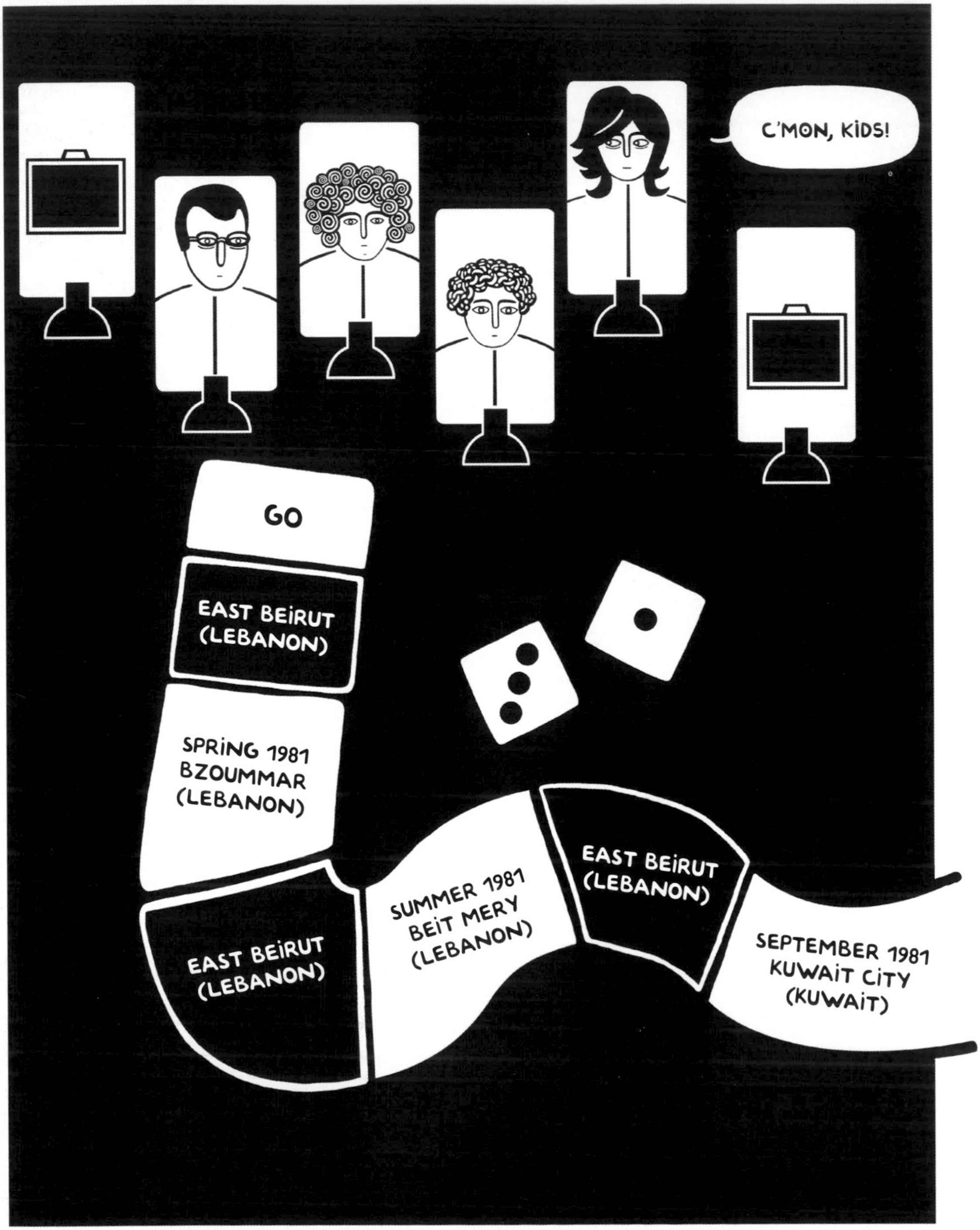
C'MON, KIDS!
GO
EAST BEIRUT (LEBANON)
SPRING 1981 BZOUMMAR (LEBANON)
EAST BEIRUT (LEBANON)
SUMMER 1981 BEIT MERY (LEBANON)
EAST BEIRUT (LEBANON)
SEPTEMBER 1981 KUWAIT CITY (KUWAIT)

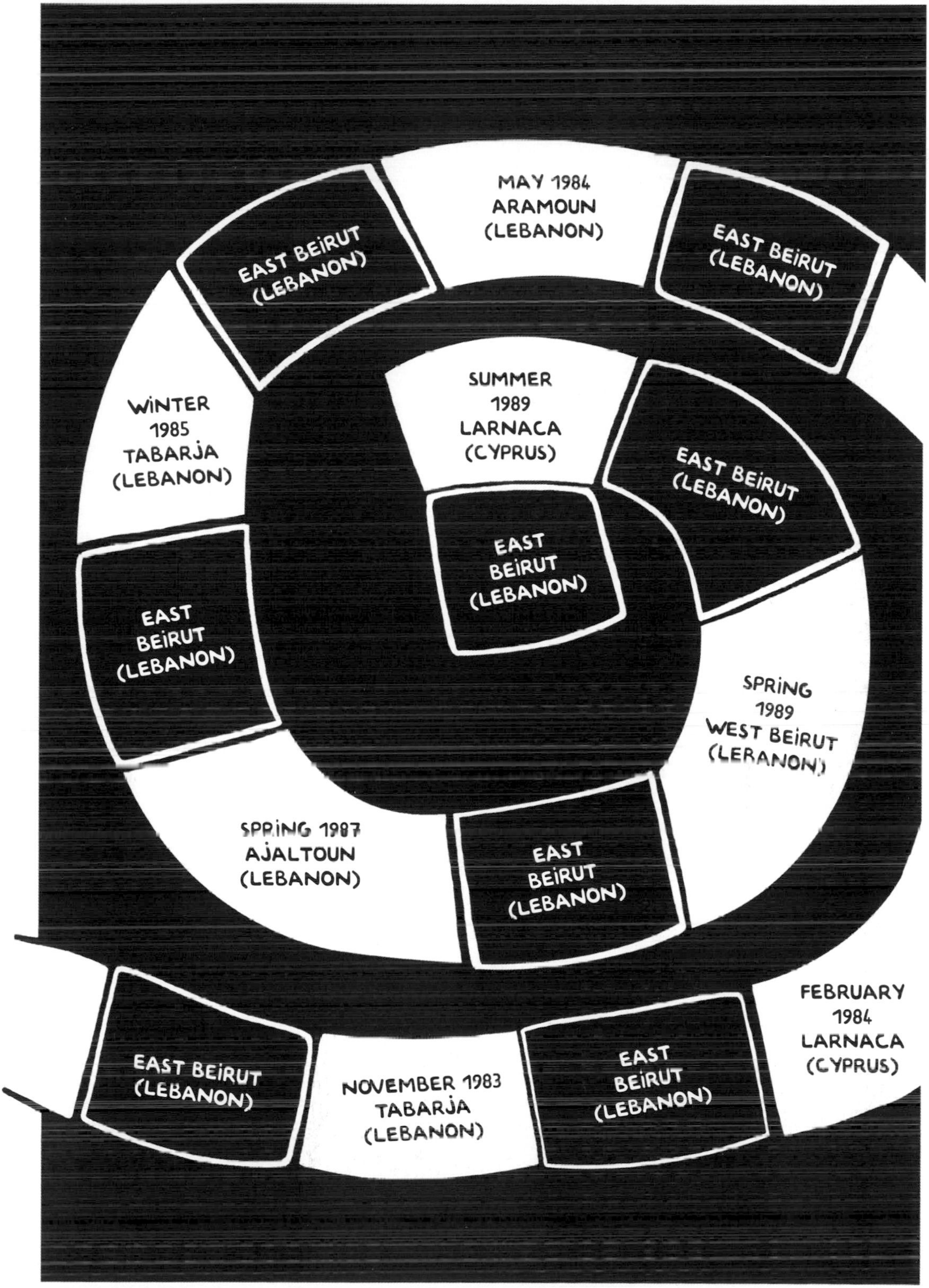
EAST BEIRUT (LEBANON)
NOVEMBER 1983 TABARJA (LEBANON)
EAST BEIRUT (LEBANON)
FEBRUARY 1984 LARNACA (CYPRUS)
EAST BEIRUT (LEBANON)
MAY 1984 ARAMOUN (LEBANON)
EAST BEIRUT (LEBANON)
WINTER 1985 TABARJA (LEBANON)
EAST BEIRUT (LEBANON)
SPRING 1987 AJALTOUN (LEBANON)
EAST BEIRUT (LEBANON)
SPRING 1989 WEST BEIRUT (LEBANON)
EAST BEIRUT (LEBANON)
SUMMER 1989 LARNACA (CYPRUS)
EAST BEIRUT (LEBANON)

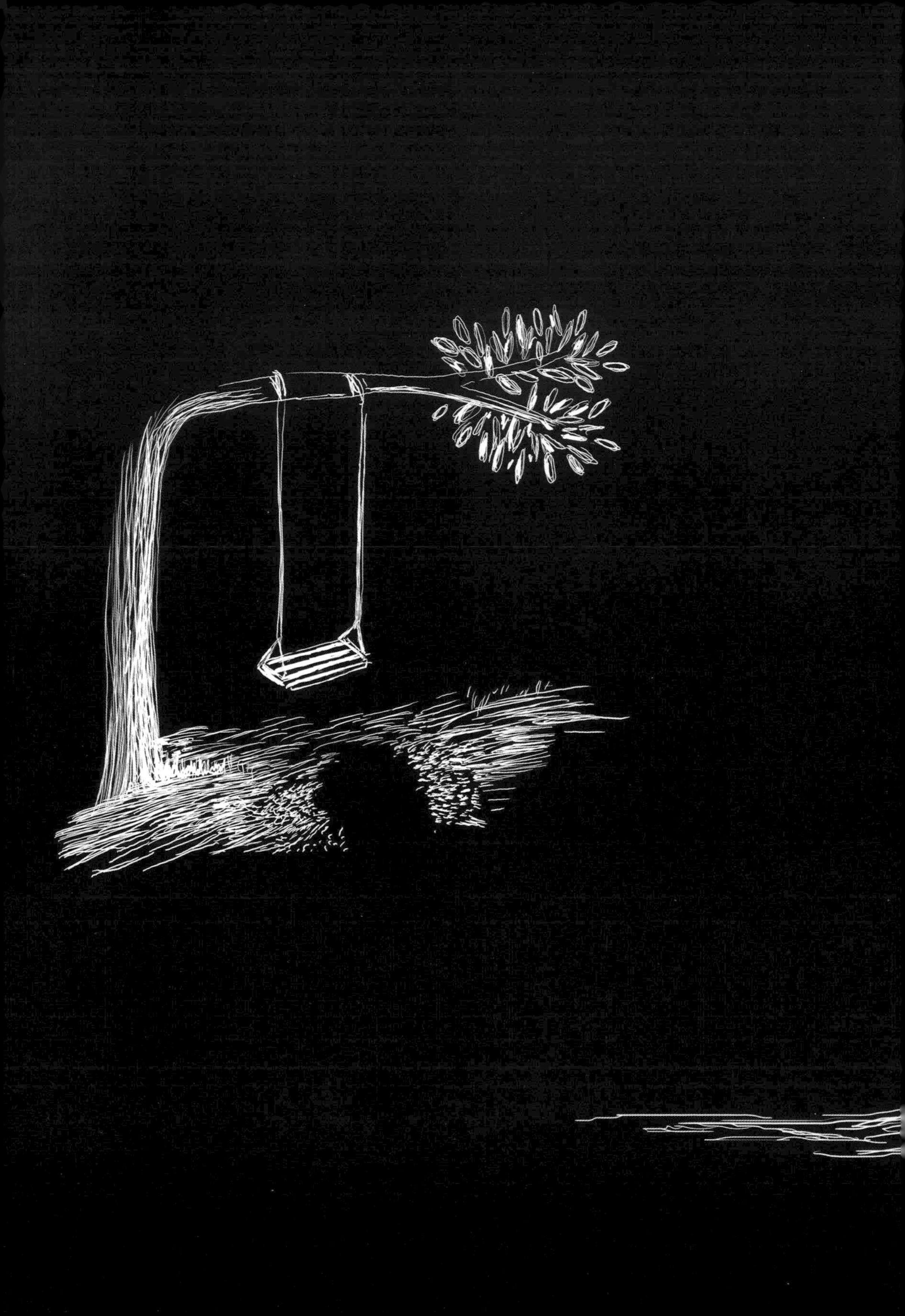

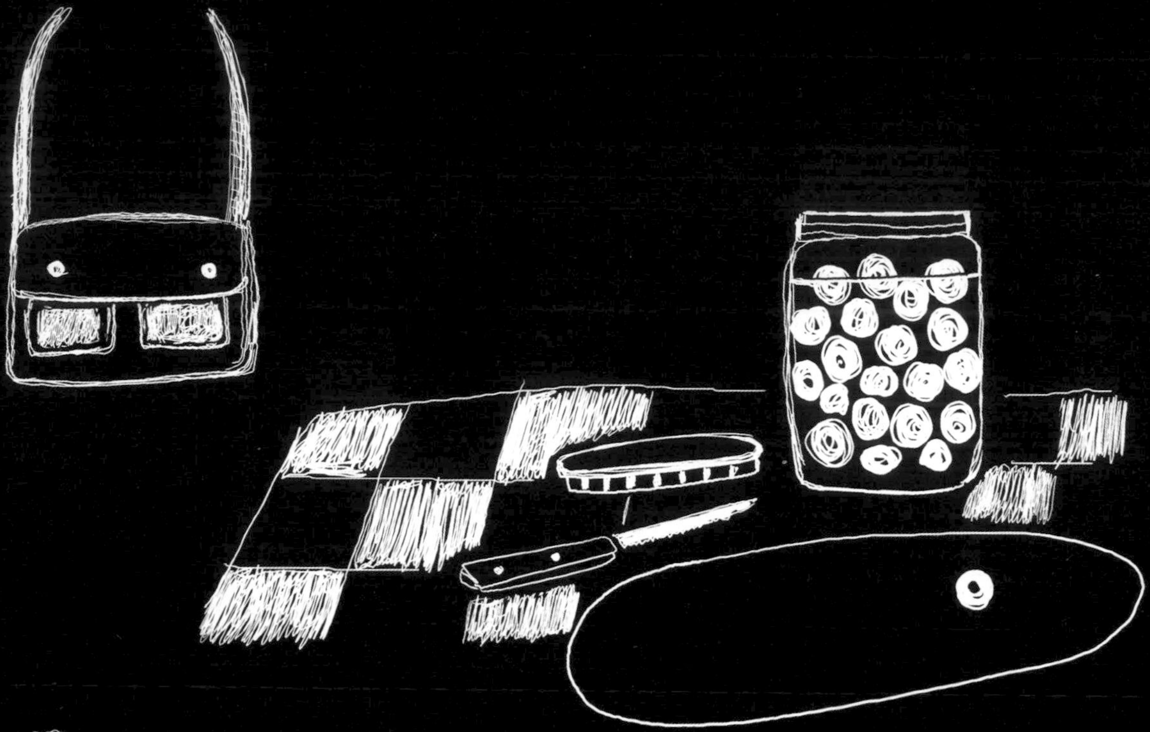

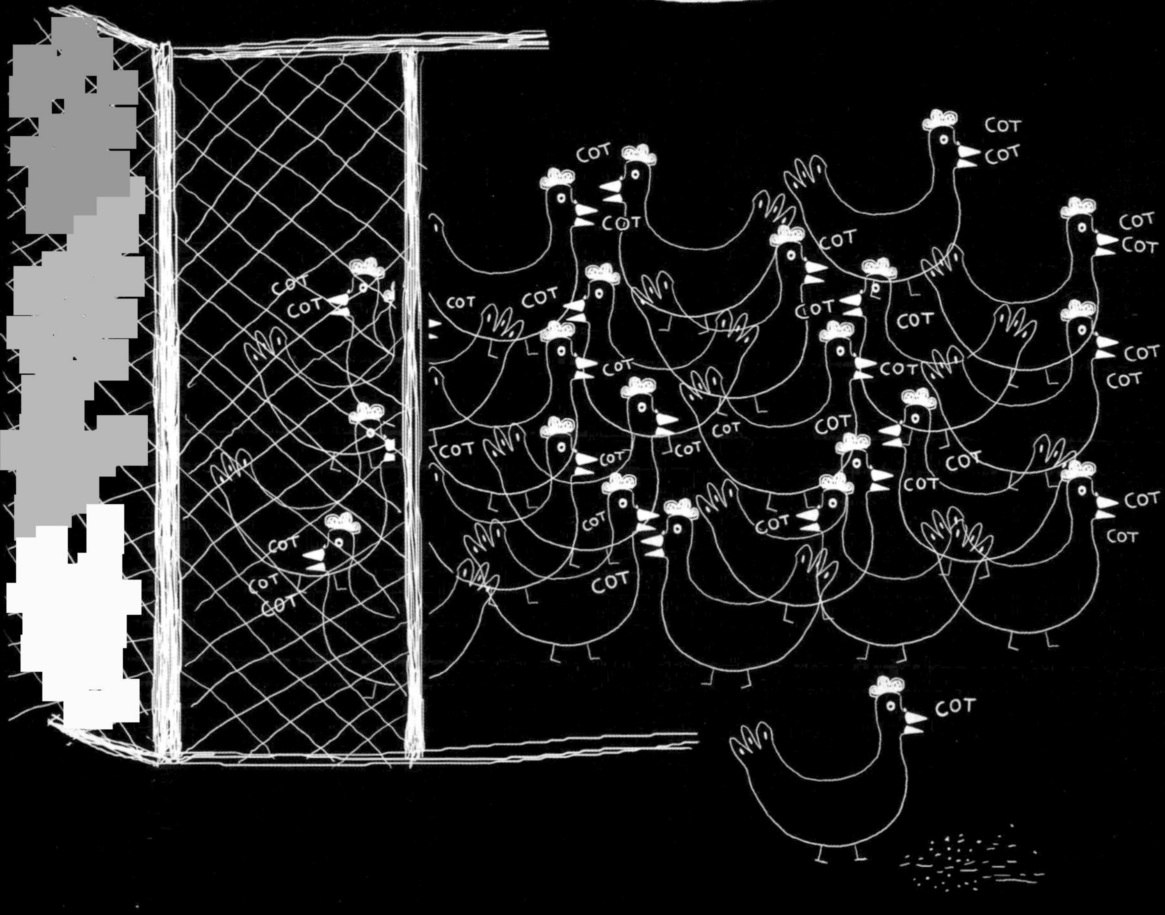
COT
COT COT
COT
COT
COT
COT COT
COT COT
COT
COT
COT
COT
COT
COT
COT
COT
COT
COT
COT
COT
COT
COT
COT
COT
COT
COT
COT
COT
COT
COT COT
COT
COT
COT COT
COT

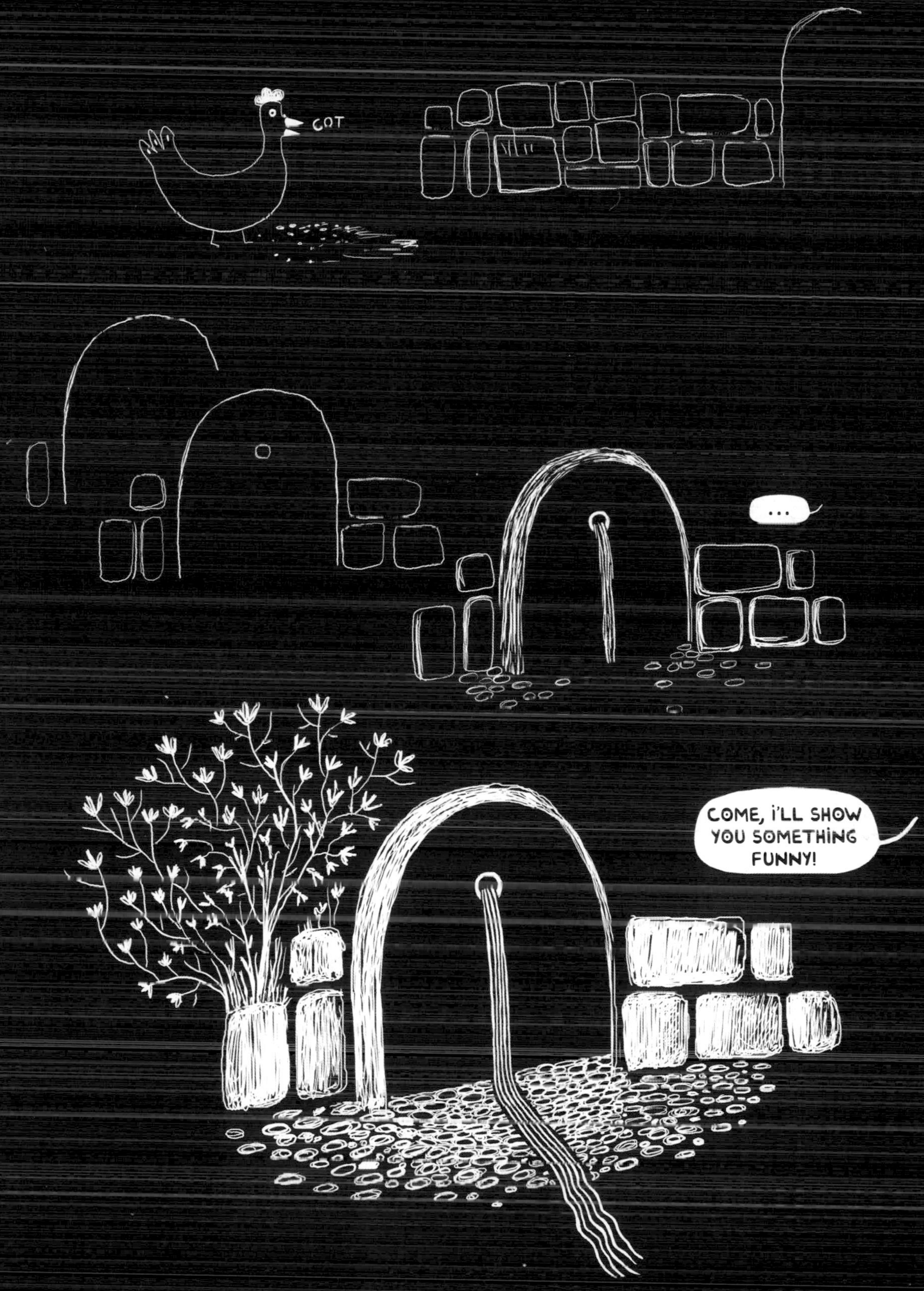
COT
...
COME, I'LL SHOW YOU SOMETHING FUNNY!

I REMEMBER HOW TO FOLD A PAPER BOAT:

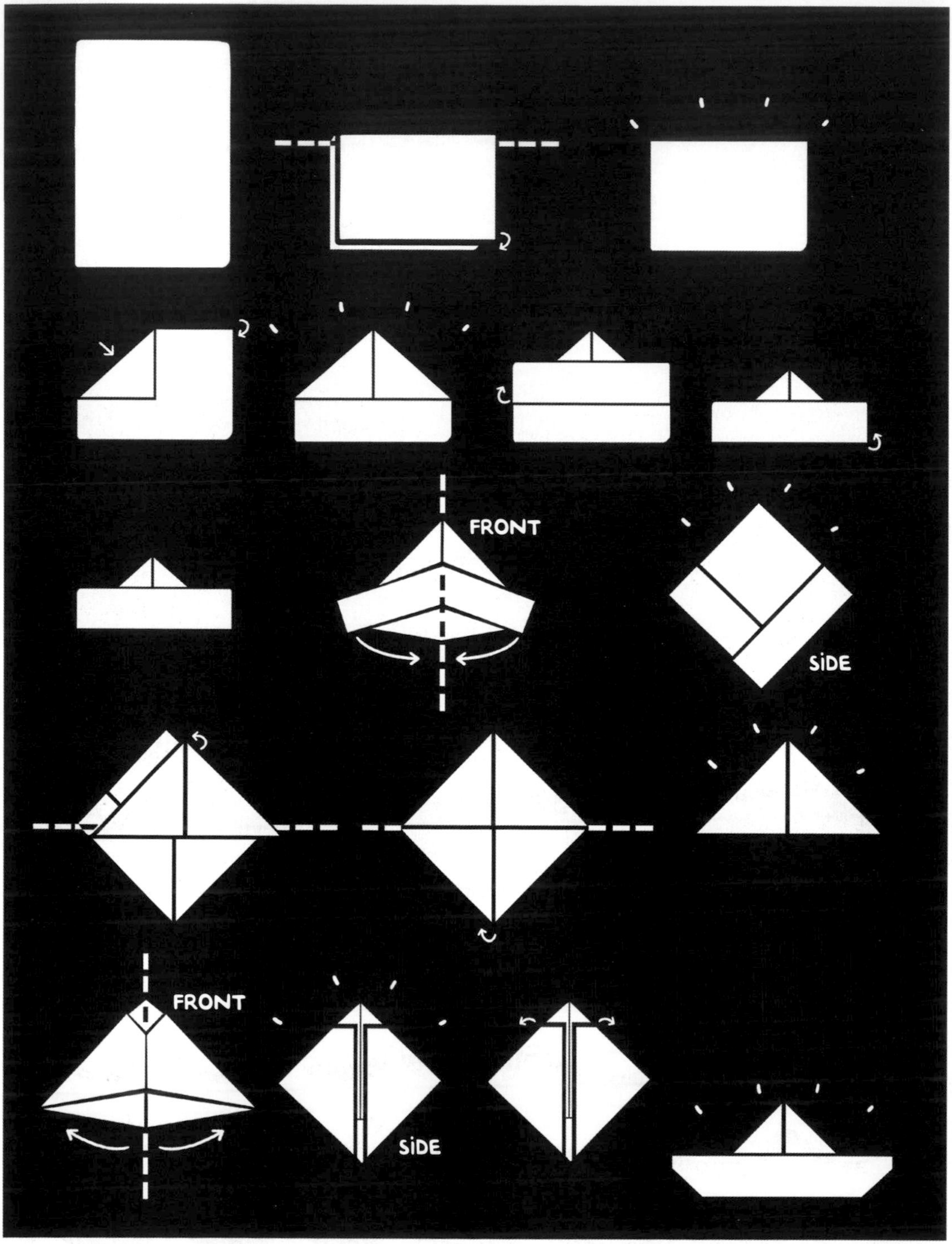
FRONT
SIDE
FRONT
SIDE

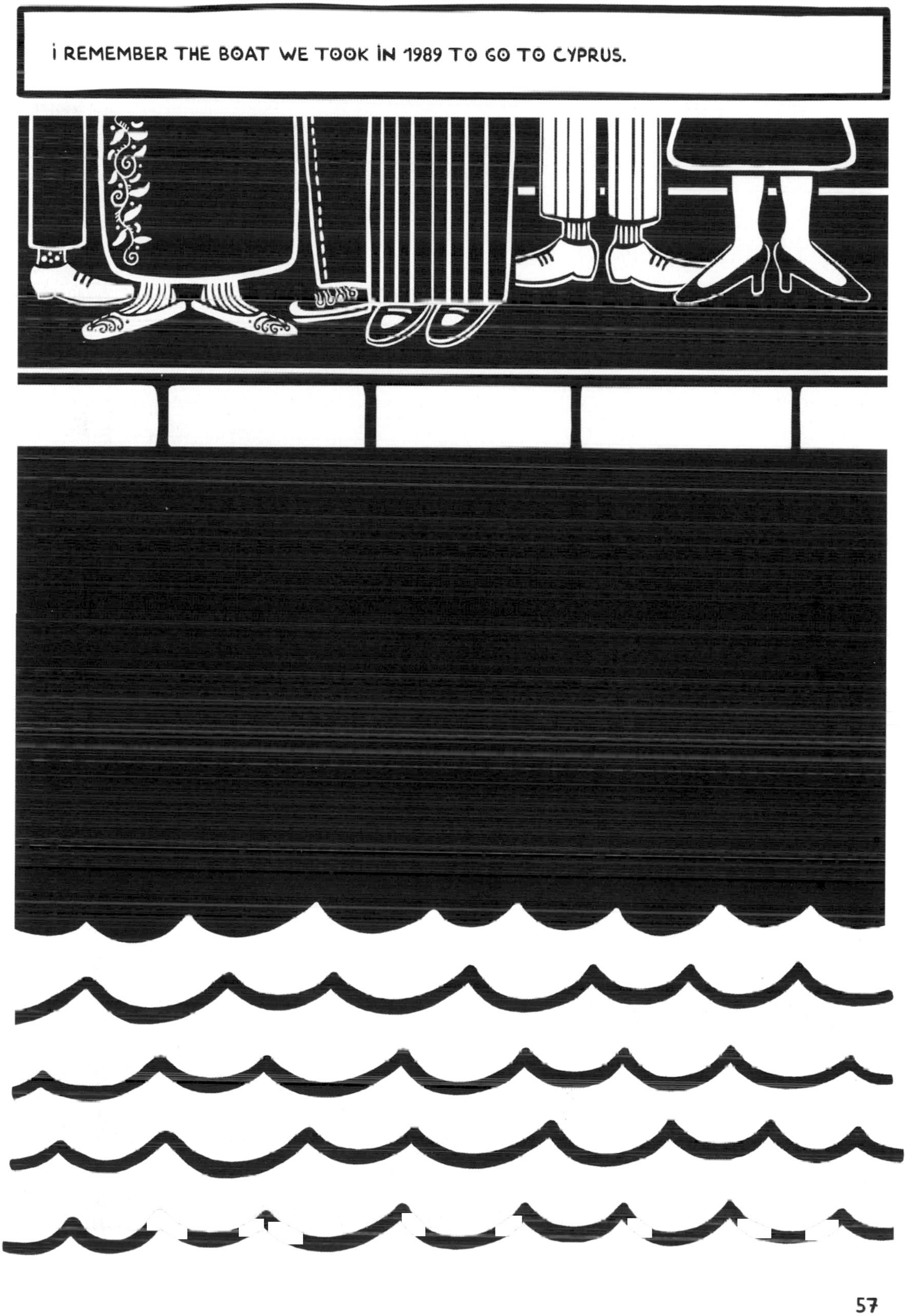
I REMEMBER THE BOAT WE TOOK IN 1989 TO GO TO CYPRUS.

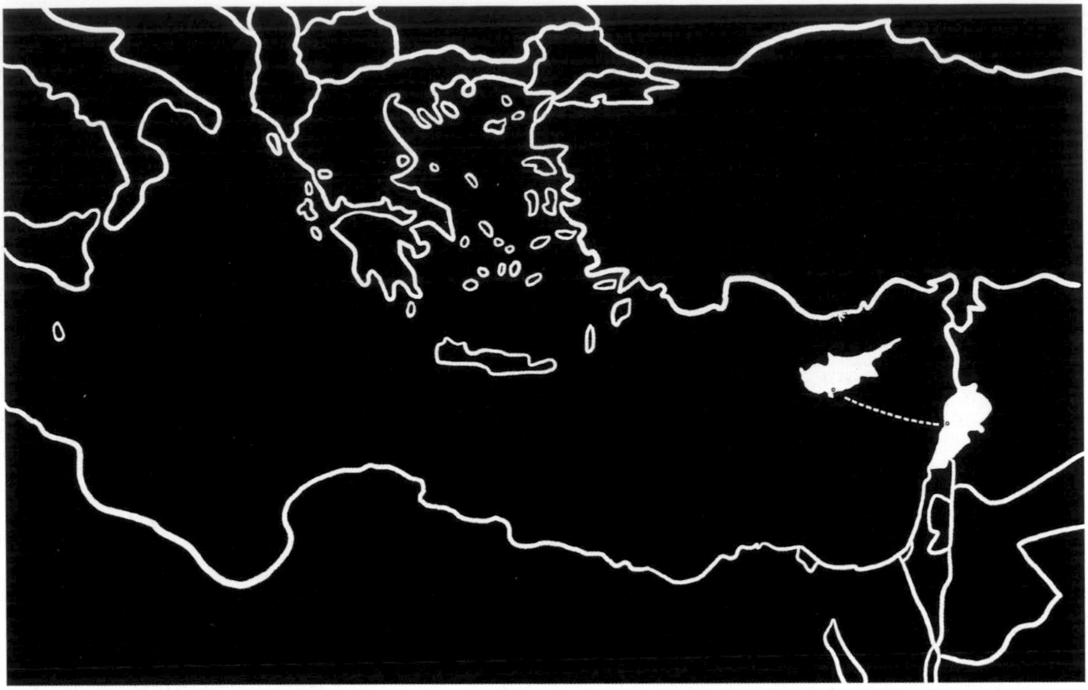

THAT YEAR, LOTS OF LEBANESE TOOK REFUGE IN LARNACA, A FEW HOURS BY BOAT FROM THE PORT OF JOUNIEH.

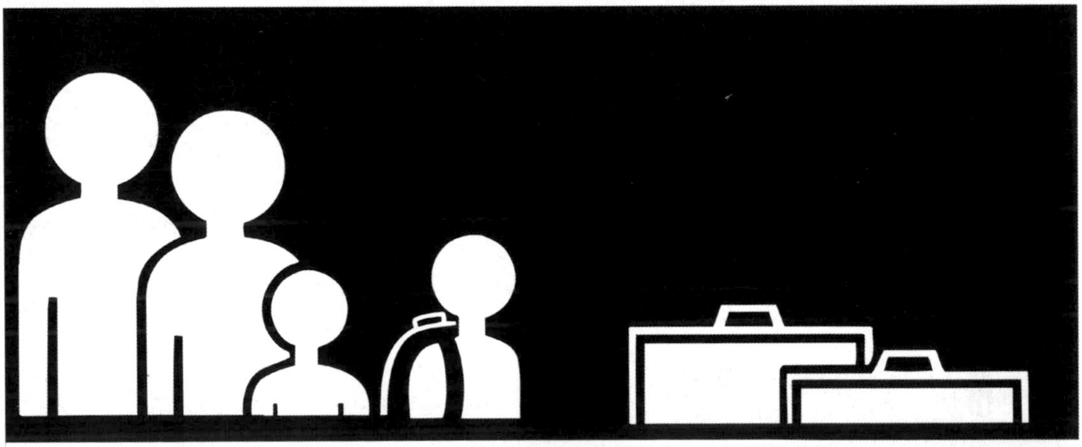

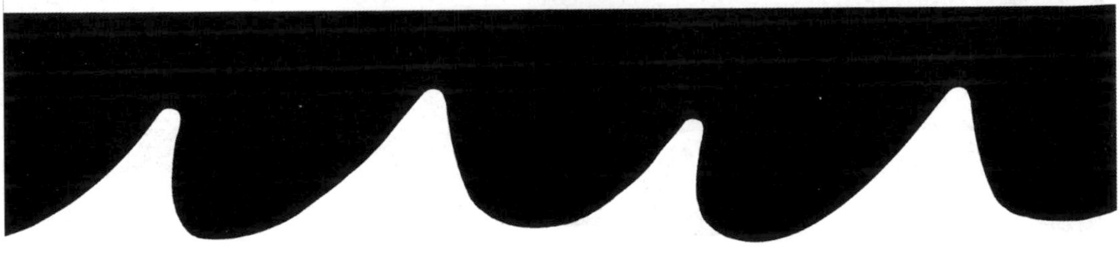

I REMEMBER THE BOAT WAS VERY BIG, AND YOU HAD TO TAKE AN INFLATABLE RAFT TO GET TO IT.

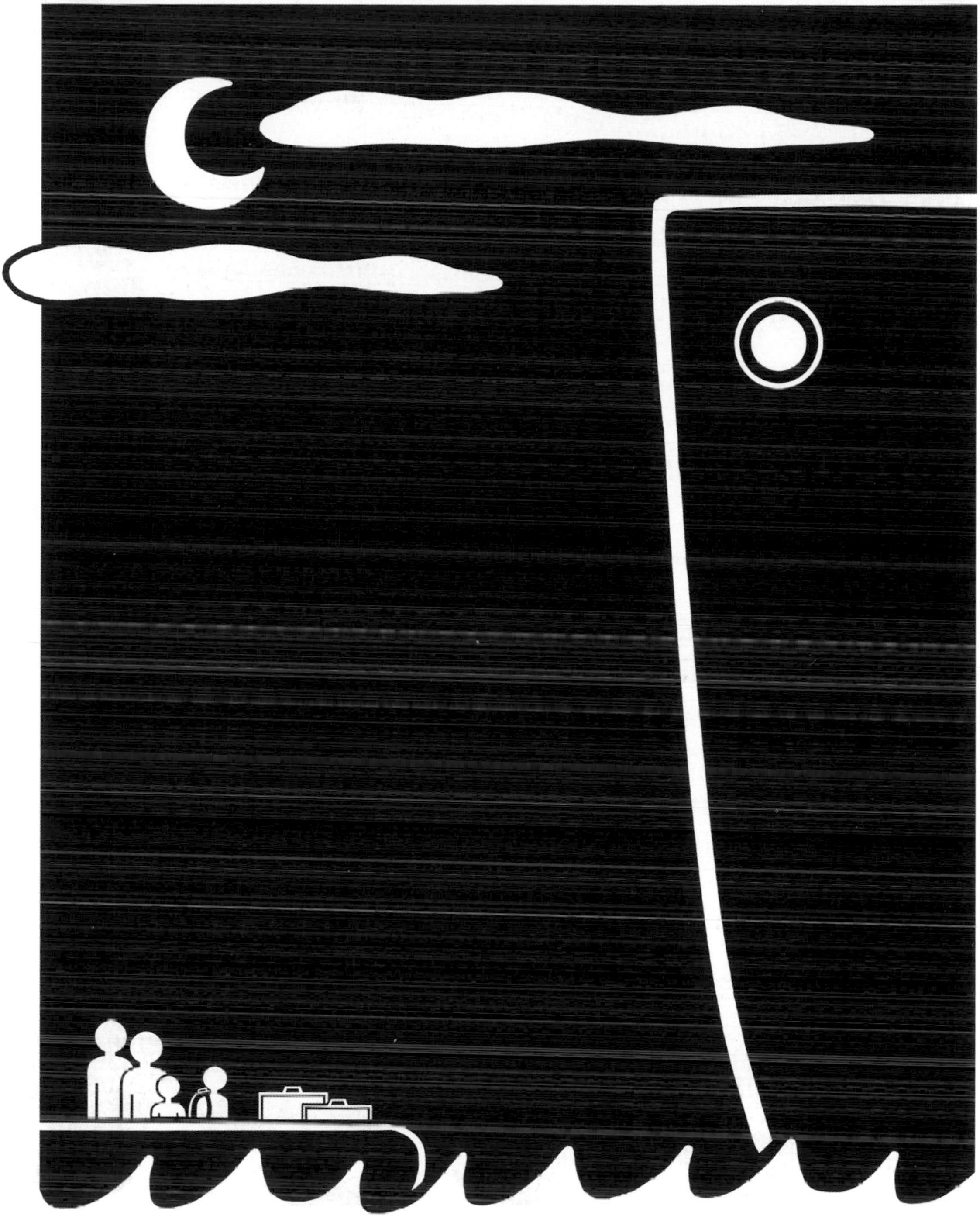

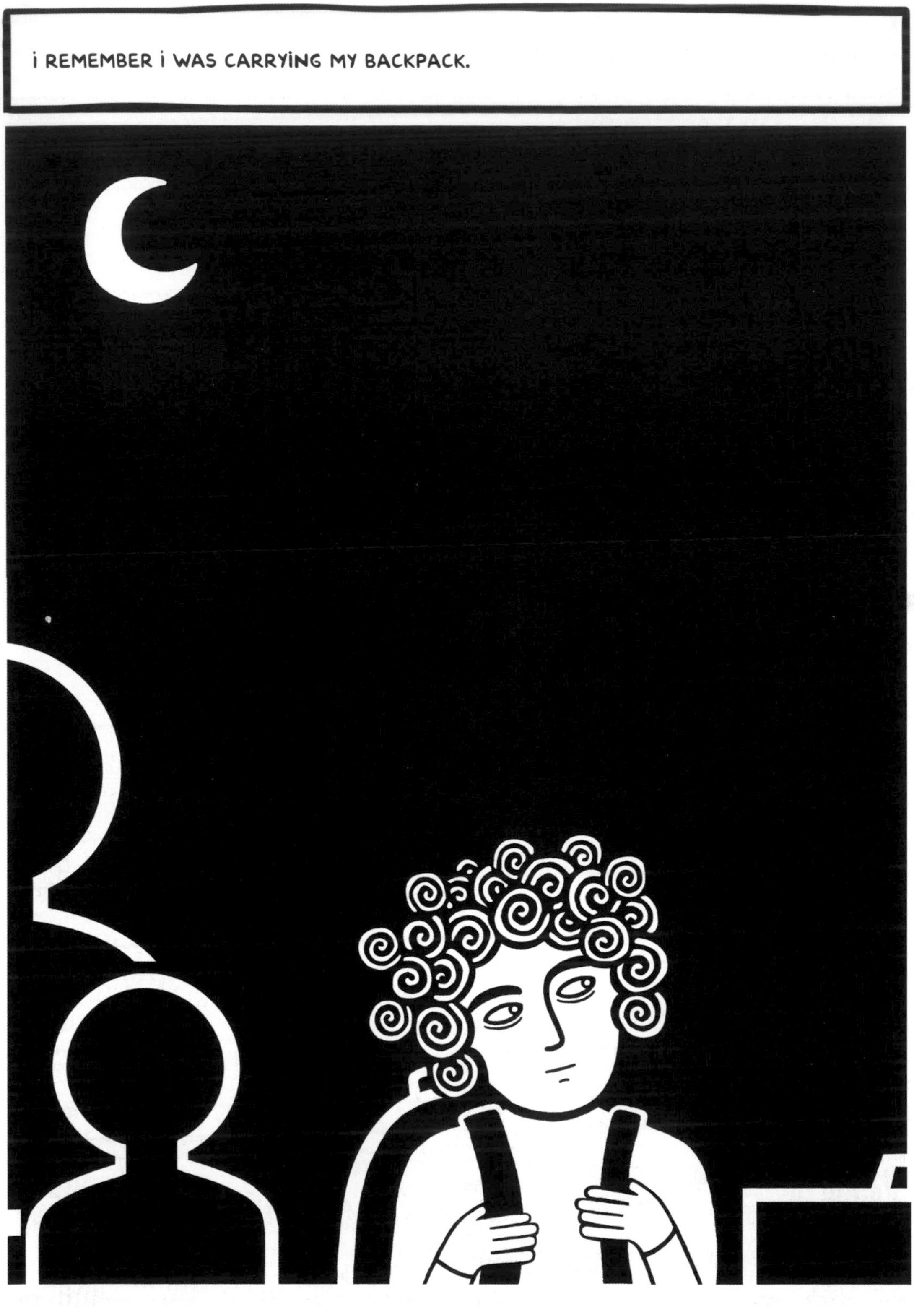
I REMEMBER I WAS CARRYING MY BACKPACK.

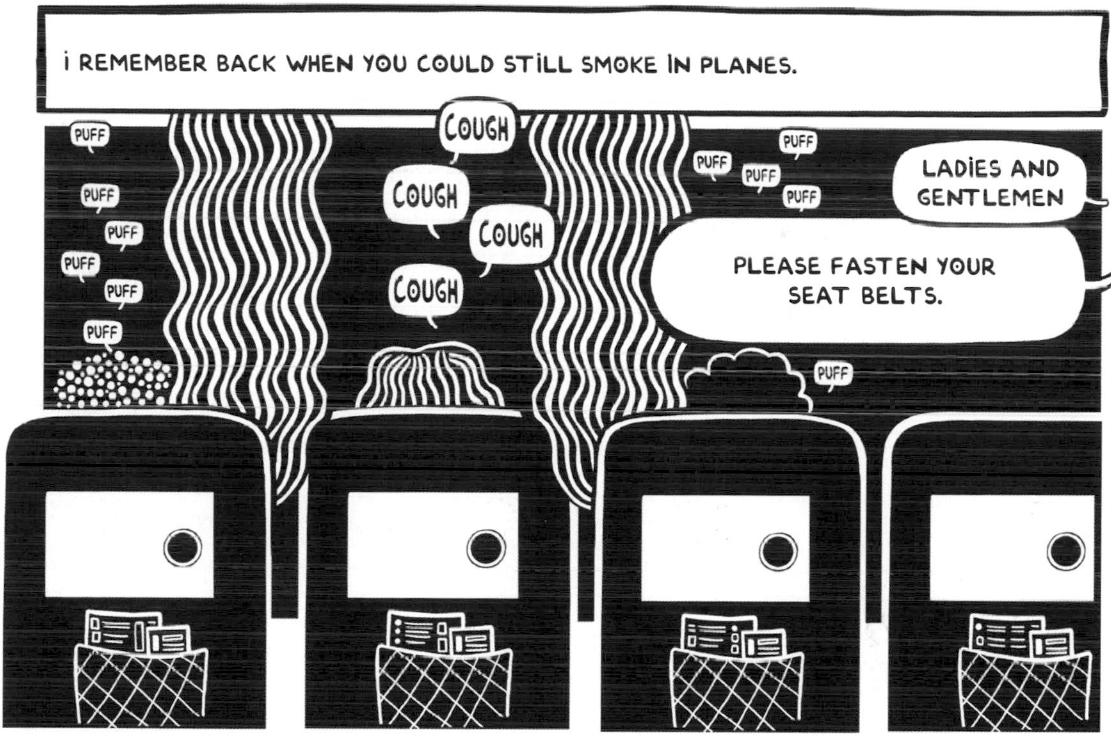
I REMEMBER BACK WHEN YOU COULD STILL SMOKE IN PLANES.
PUFF
PUFF
PUFF
PUFF
PUFF
PUFF
COUGH
COUGH
COUGH
COUGH
PUFF
PUFF
PUFF
PUFF
LADIES AND GENTLEMEN
PLEASE FASTEN YOUR SEAT BELTS.
PUFF

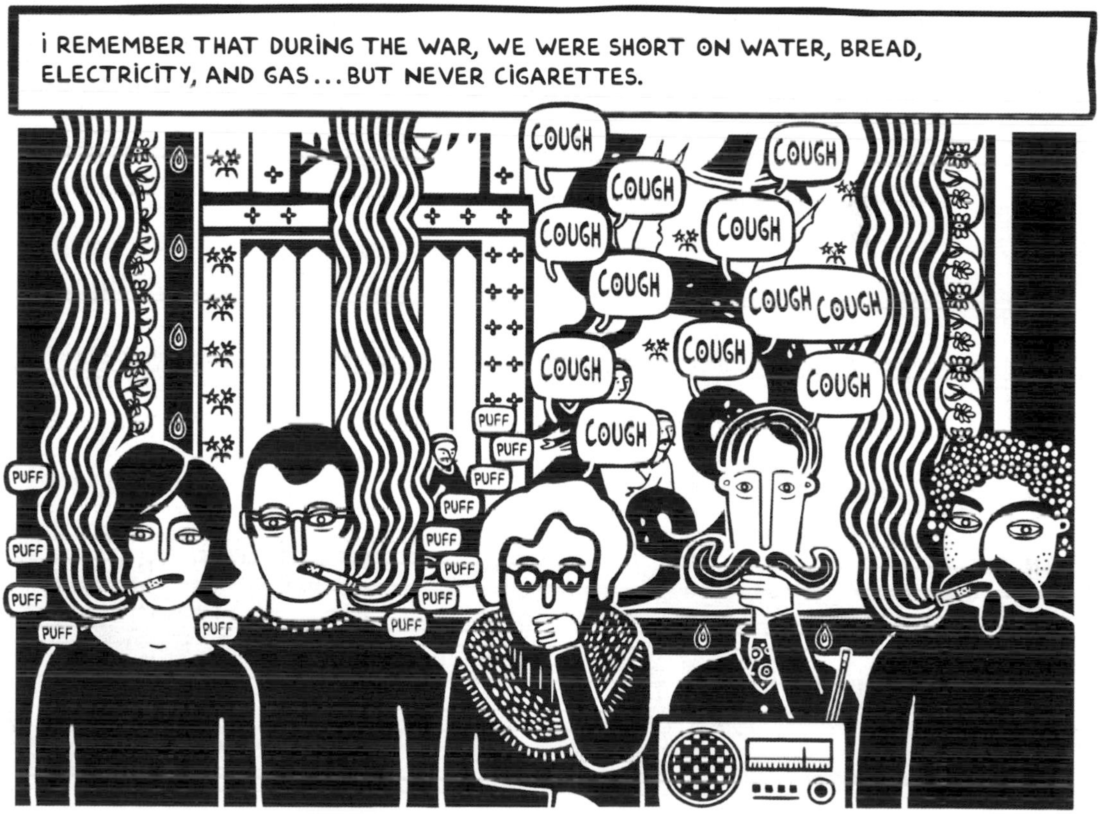
I REMEMBER THAT DURING THE WAR, WE WERE SHORT ON WATER, BREAD, ELECTRICITY, AND GAS... BUT NEVER CIGARETTES.
COUGH
COUGH
COUGH
COUGH
COUGH
COUGH
COUGH COUGH
COUGH
COUGH
COUGH
COUGH
PUFF
PUFF
PUFF
PUFF
PUFF
PUFF
PUFF
PUFF
PUFF
PUFF
PUFF
PUFF
PUFF
PUFF

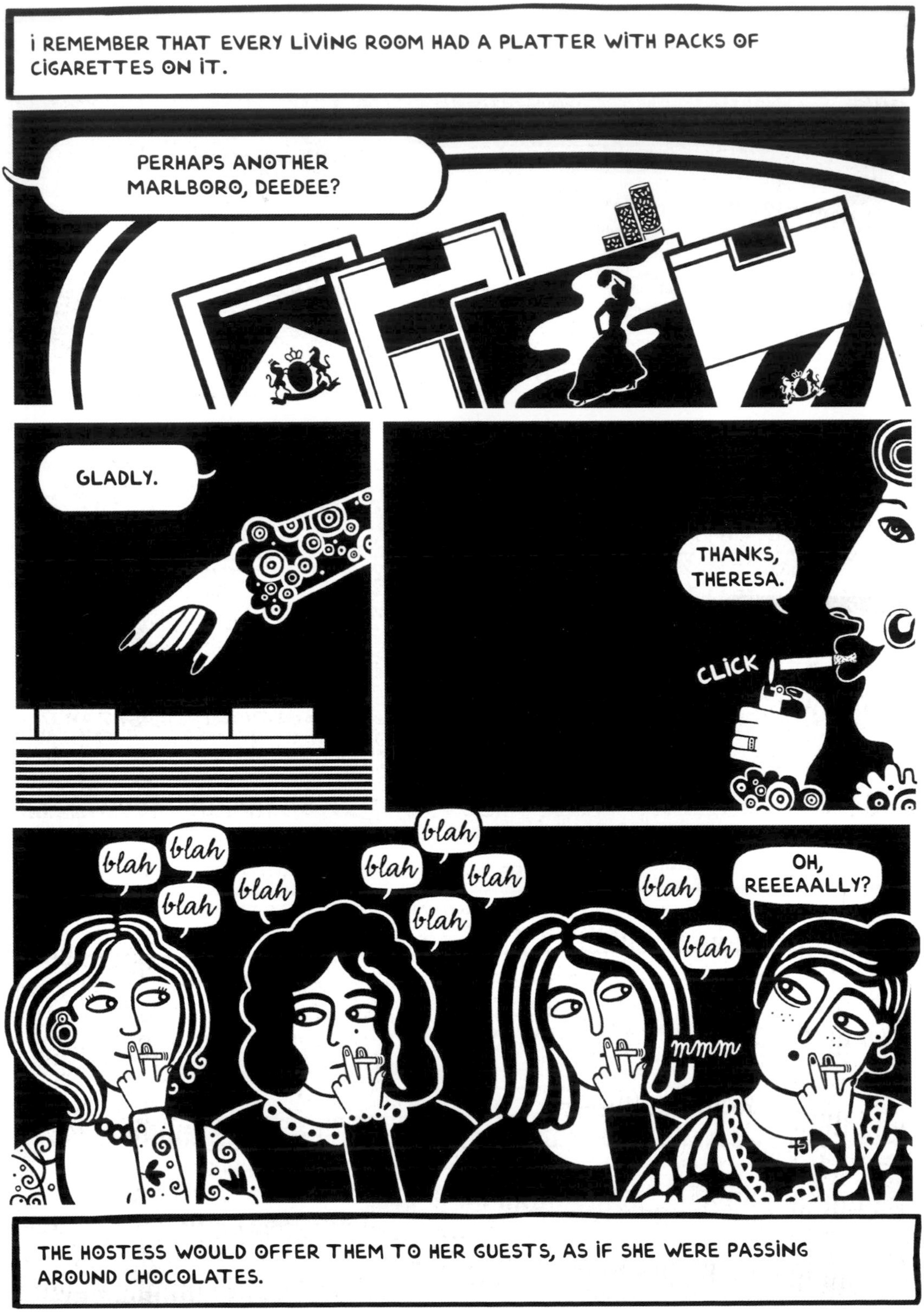
I REMEMBER THAT EVERY LIVING ROOM HAD A PLATTER WITH PACKS OF CIGARETTES ON IT.
PERHAPS ANOTHER MARLBORO, DEEDEE?
GLADLY.
THANKS, THERESA.
CLICK
blah
blah
blah
blah
blah
blah
blah
blah
blah
blah
OH, REEEAALLY?
mmm
THE HOSTESS WOULD OFFER THEM TO HER GUESTS, AS IF SHE WERE PASSING AROUND CHOCOLATES.

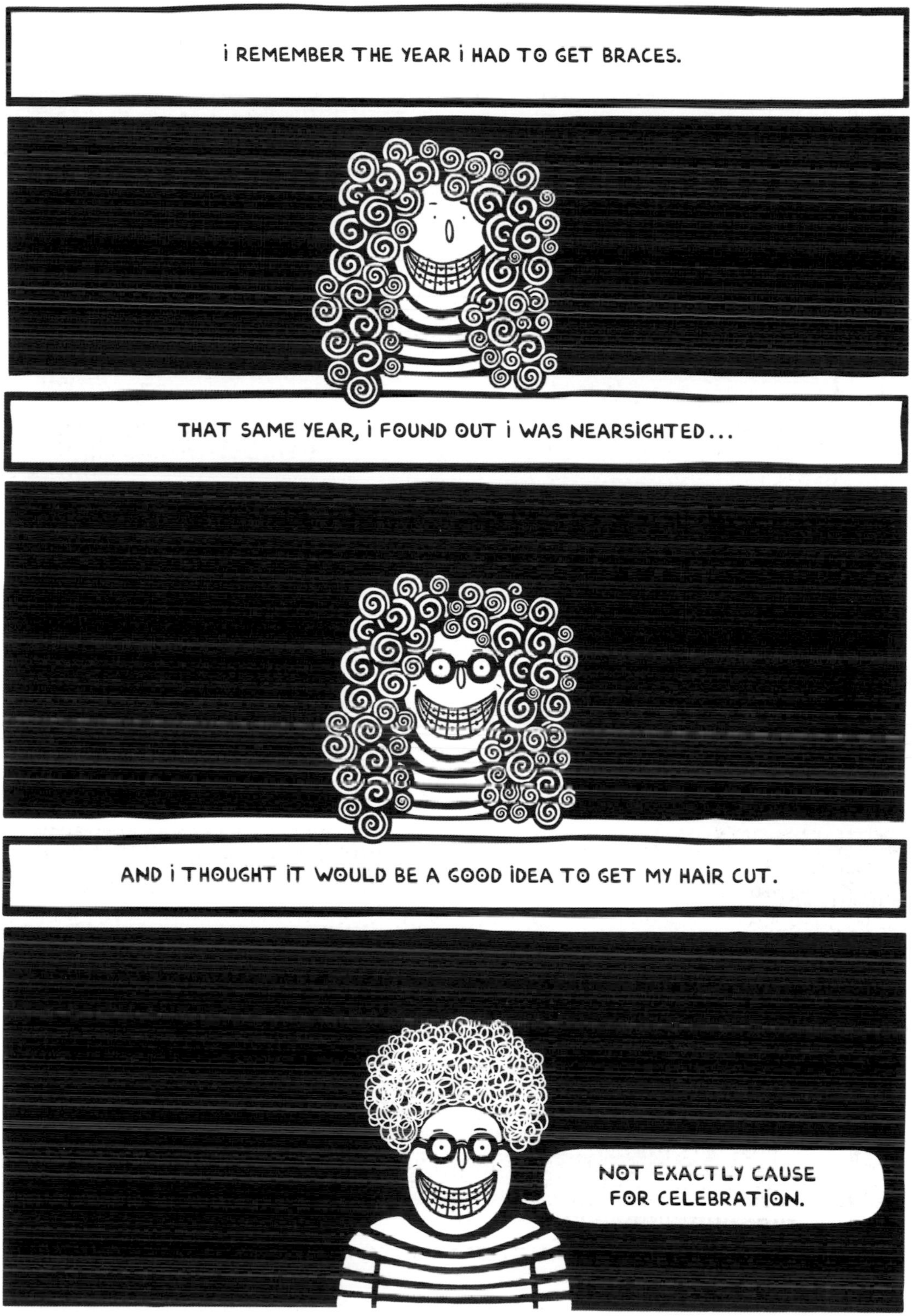
i REMEMBER THE YEAR i HAD TO GET BRACES.
THAT SAME YEAR, i FOUND OUT i WAS NEARSiGHTED...
AND i THOUGHT iT WOULD BE A GOOD iDEA TO GET MY HAiR CUT.
NOT EXACTLY CAUSE FOR CELEBRATiON.

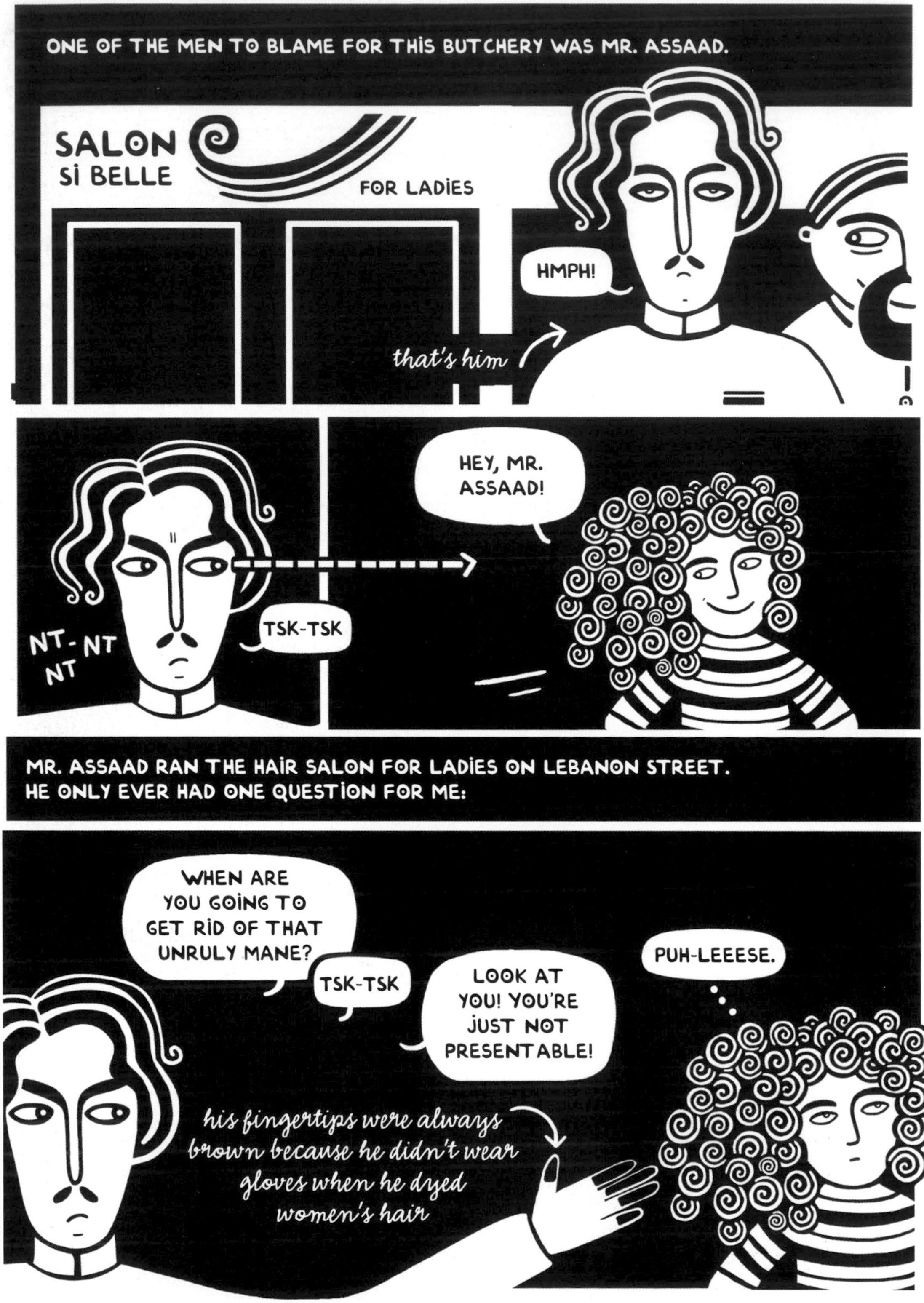

ONE OF THE MEN TO BLAME FOR THIS BUTCHERY WAS MR. ASSAAD.
SALON Si BELLE
FOR LADIES
HMPH!
that's him
NT-NT NT
TSK-TSK
HEY, MR. ASSAAD!
MR. ASSAAD RAN THE HAIR SALON FOR LADIES ON LEBANON STREET. HE ONLY EVER HAD ONE QUESTION FOR ME:
WHEN ARE YOU GOING TO GET RID OF THAT UNRULY MANE?
TSK-TSK
LOOK AT YOU! YOU'RE JUST NOT PRESENTABLE!
PUH-LEEESE.
his fingertips were always brown because he didn't wear gloves when he dyed women's hair

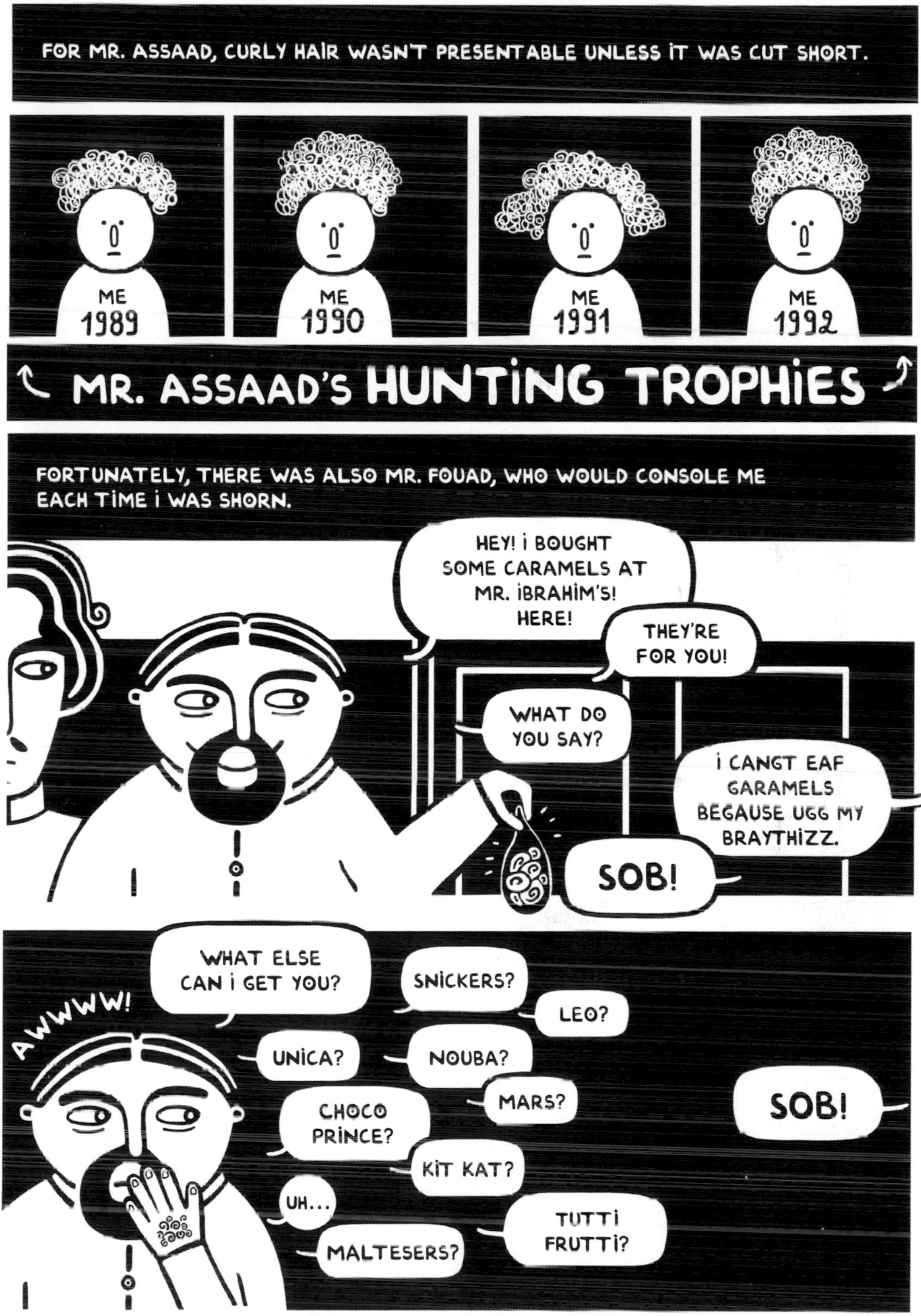
FOR MR. ASSAAD, CURLY HAIR WASN'T PRESENTABLE UNLESS IT WAS CUT SHORT.
ME 1989
ME 1990
ME 1991
ME 1992
MR. ASSAAD'S HUNTING TROPHIES
FORTUNATELY, THERE WAS ALSO MR. FOUAD, WHO WOULD CONSOLE ME EACH TIME I WAS SHORN.
HEY! I BOUGHT SOME CARAMELS AT MR. IBRAHIM'S! HERE!
THEY'RE FOR YOU!
WHAT DO YOU SAY?
I CANGT EAF GARAMELS BEGAUSE UGG MY BRAYTHIZZ.
SOB!
AWWWW!
WHAT ELSE CAN I GET YOU?
SNICKERS?
LEO?
UNICA?
NOUBA?
MARS?
CHOCO PRINCE?
KIT KAT?
UH...
TUTTI FRUTTI?
MALTESERS?
SOB!

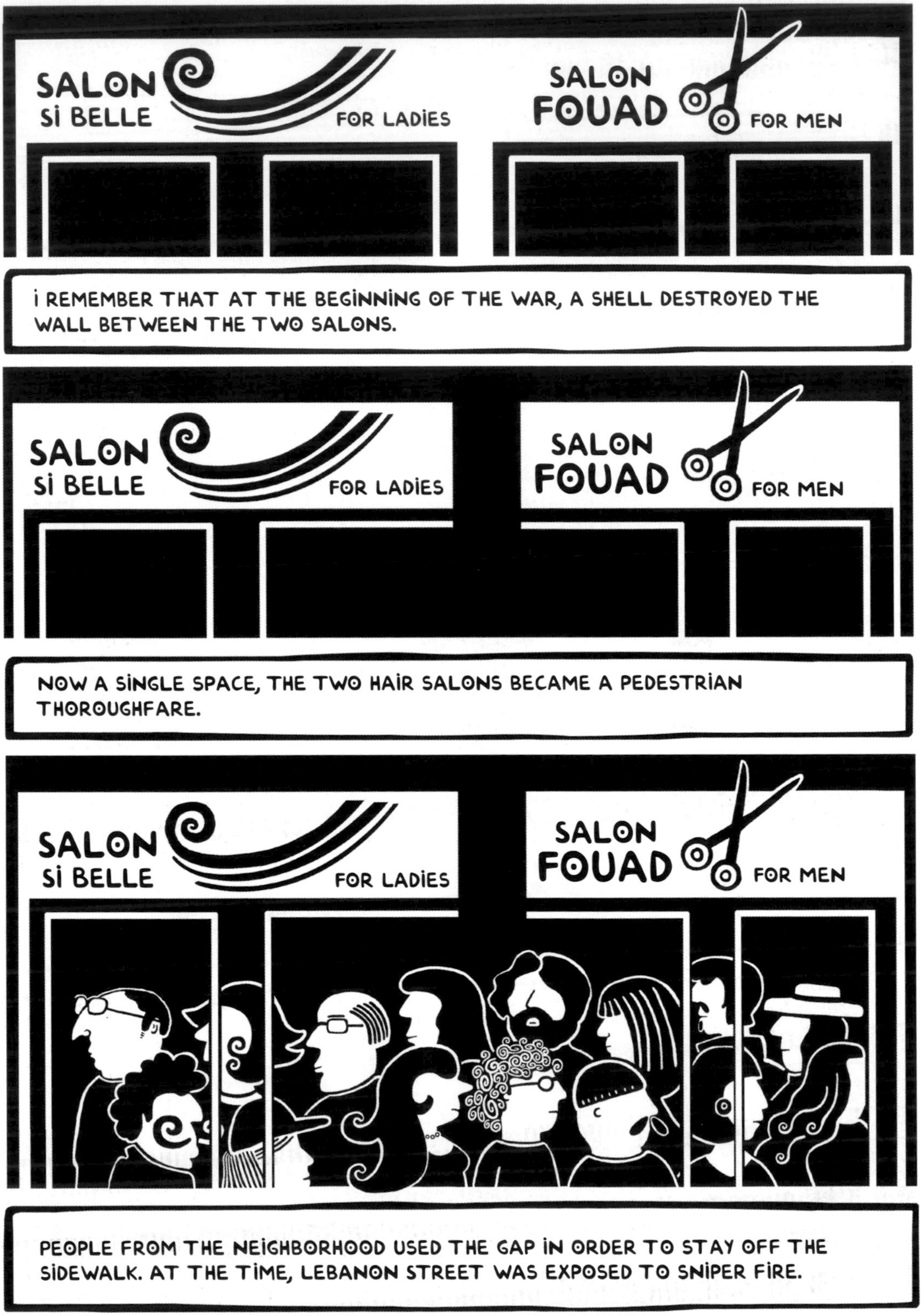
SALON Si BELLE
FOR LADiES
SALON FOUAD
FOR MEN
i REMEMBER THAT AT THE BEGiNNiNG OF THE WAR, A SHELL DESTROYED THE WALL BETWEEN THE TWO SALONS.
SALON Si BELLE
FOR LADiES
SALON FOUAD
FOR MEN
NOW A SiNGLE SPACE, THE TWO HAiR SALONS BECAME A PEDESTRiAN THOROUGHFARE.
SALON Si BELLE
FOR LADiES
SALON FOUAD
FOR MEN
PEOPLE FROM THE NEiGHBORHOOD USED THE GAP iN ORDER TO STAY OFF THE SiDEWALK. AT THE TiME, LEBANON STREET WAS EXPOSED TO SNiPER FiRE.

AFTER THE WAR, THE WALL WAS REBUILT.

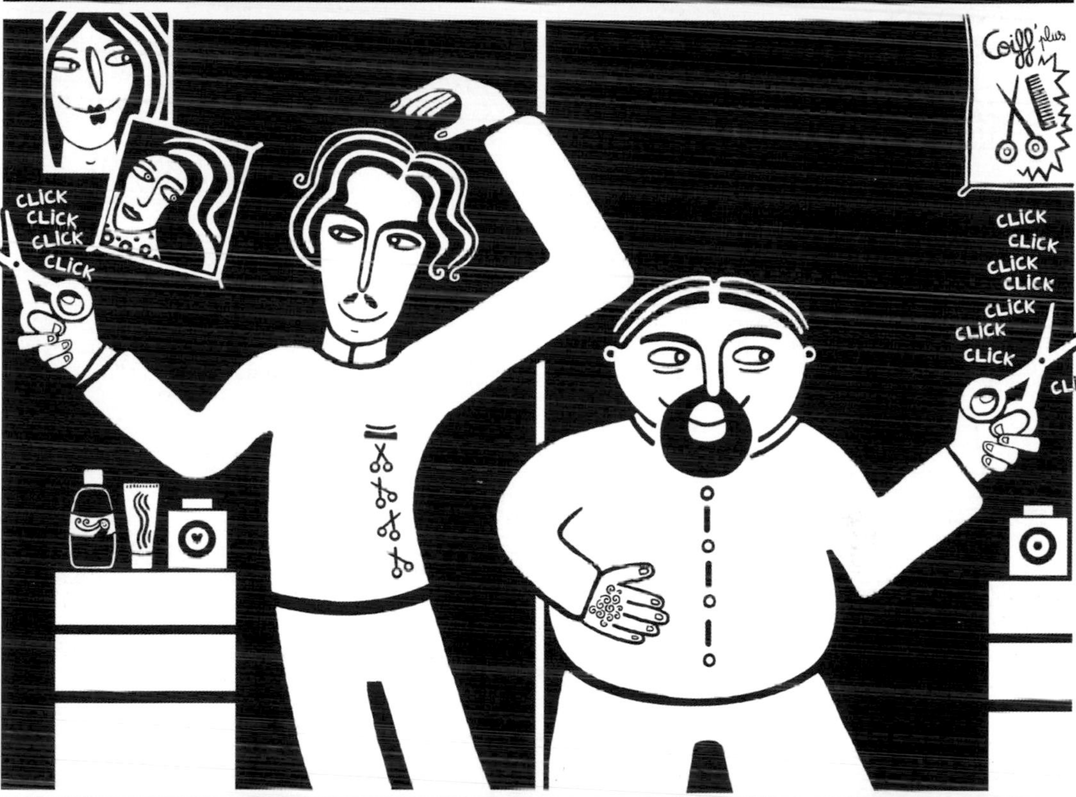
CLICK
CLICK
CLICK
CLICK
Coiff' plus
CLICK
CLICK
CLICK
CLICK
CLICK
CLICK
CLICK
CLICK

LOCALS STARTED USING THE SIDEWALK AGAIN.

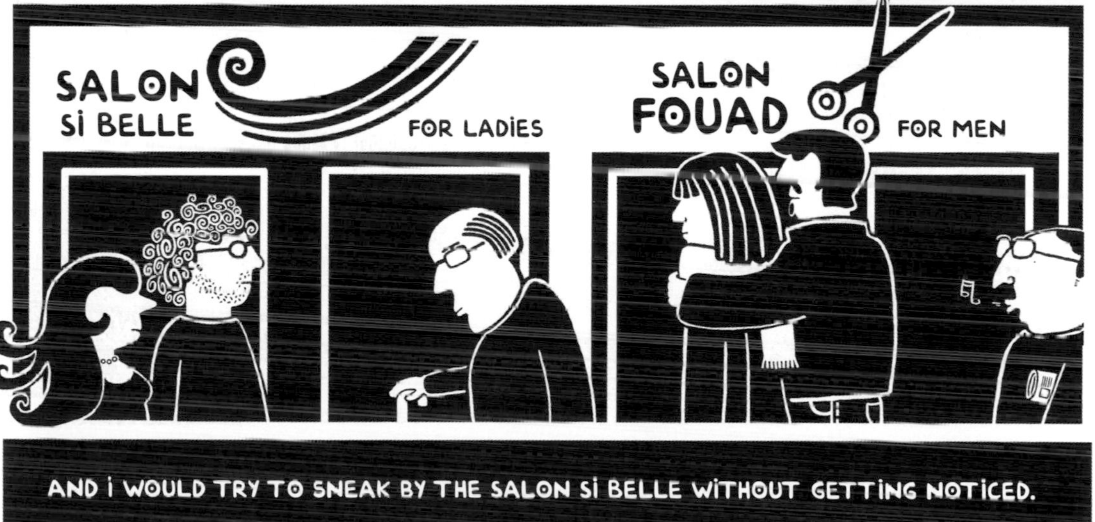
SALON
SI BELLE
FOR LADIES
SALON
FOUAD
FOR MEN

AND I WOULD TRY TO SNEAK BY THE SALON SI BELLE WITHOUT GETTING NOTICED.

I REMEMBER OLD KIT KAT WRAPPERS.

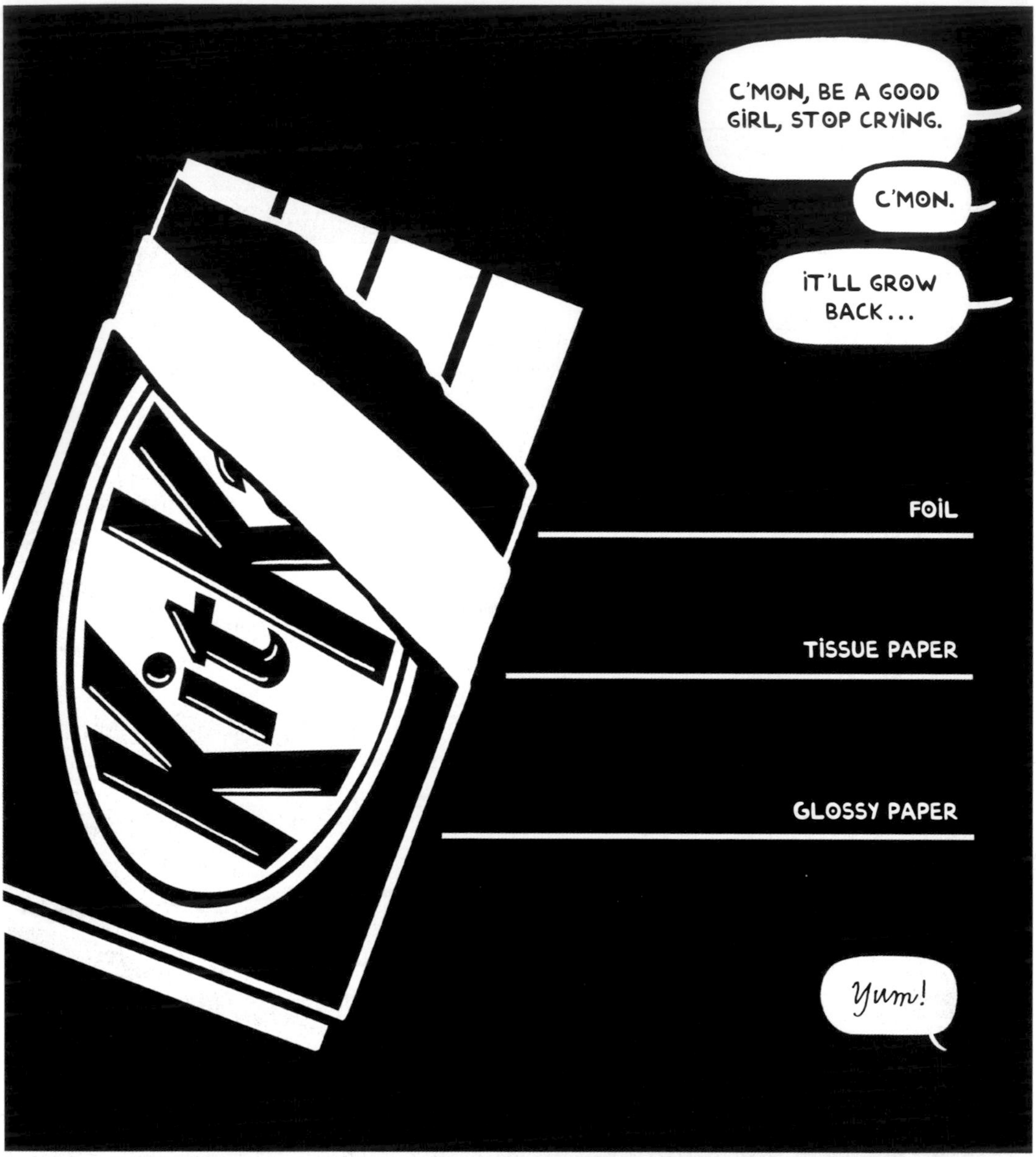
C'MON, BE A GOOD GIRL, STOP CRYING.
C'MON.
IT'LL GROW BACK...
KitKat
FOIL
TISSUE PAPER
GLOSSY PAPER
Yum!

I REMEMBER THE THREE STEPS BEFORE EATING: RIPPING THROUGH THE GLOSSY RED PAPER, FOLDING BACK THE WHITE TISSUE PAPER, AND CRINKLING UP THE FOIL. SOMETIMES THE CHOCOLATE WOULD STICK TO THE FOIL A LITTLE.

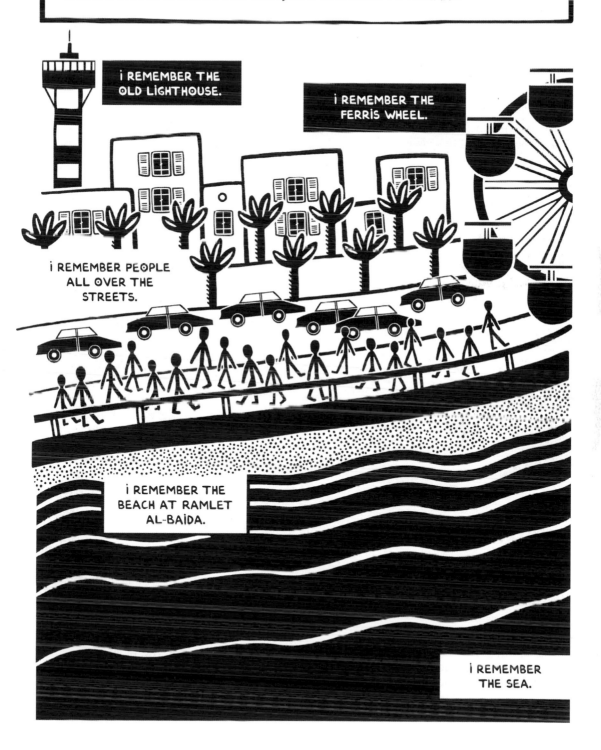

I REMEMBER THE FIRST TIME I WENT TO WEST BEIRUT. IT WAS 1989, WHEN THE WAR HAD MOVED EAST. IN THE WEST, LIFE WAS BACK TO NORMAL.

I REMEMBER THE OLD LIGHTHOUSE.

I REMEMBER THE FERRIS WHEEL.

I REMEMBER PEOPLE ALL OVER THE STREETS.

I REMEMBER THE BEACH AT RAMLET AL-BAIDA.

I REMEMBER THE SEA.

THAT MORNING, THE SITUATION WORSENED IN EAST BEIRUT. MY MOTHER QUICKLY TOSSED SOME CLOTHES IN A SUITCASE, AND WE WERE OFF.

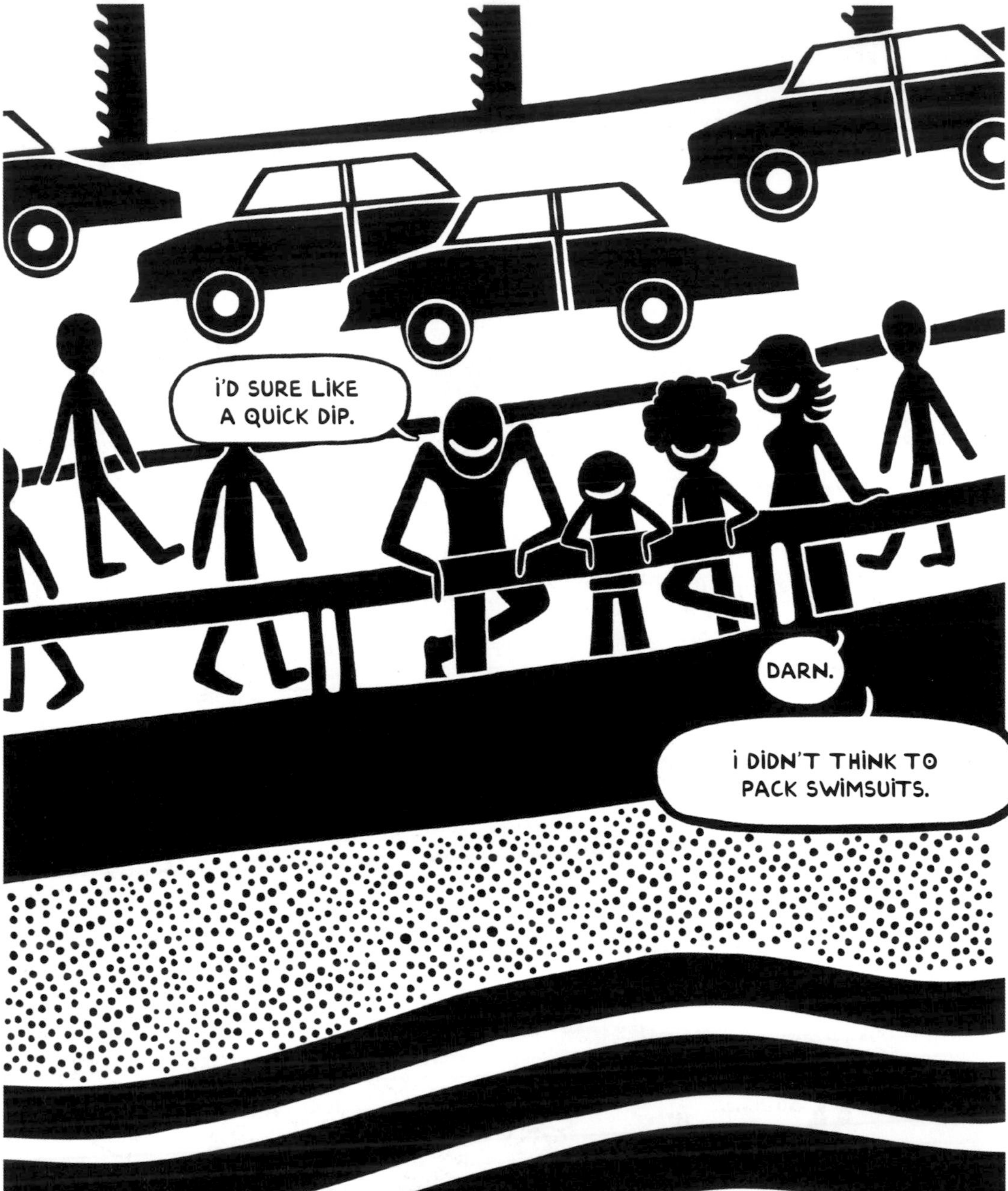
I'D SURE LIKE A QUICK DIP.
DARN.
I DIDN'T THINK TO PACK SWIMSUITS.

I REMEMBER WALKING ON THE PROMENADE IN AIN EL MREISSEH. I FELT LIKE I WAS ON VACATION.

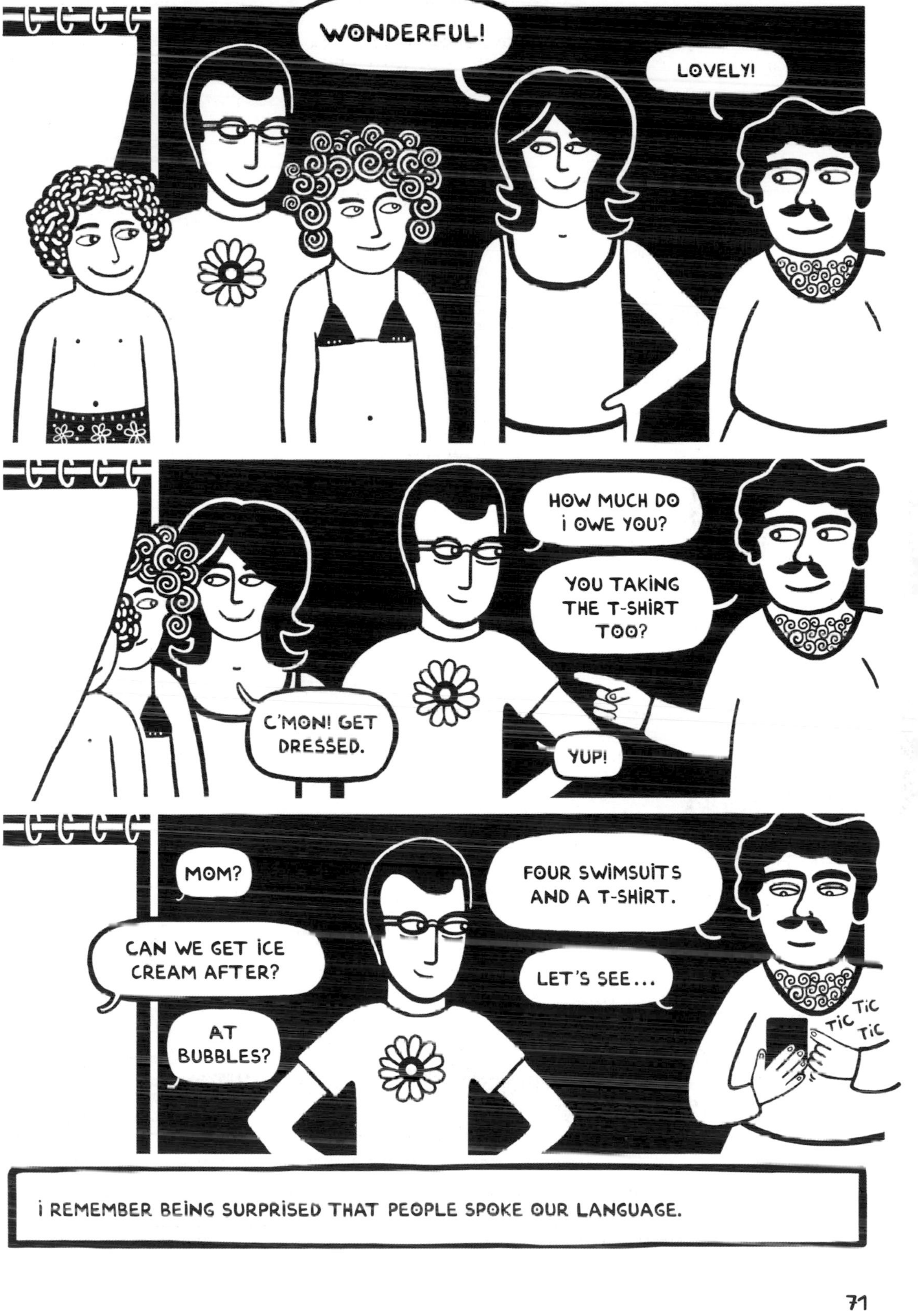
WONDERFUL!
LOVELY!
HOW MUCH DO I OWE YOU?
YOU TAKING THE T-SHIRT TOO?
C'MON! GET DRESSED.
YUP!
MOM?
FOUR SWIMSUITS AND A T-SHIRT.
CAN WE GET ICE CREAM AFTER?
LET'S SEE...
AT BUBBLES?
TIC TIC TIC
I REMEMBER BEING SURPRISED THAT PEOPLE SPOKE OUR LANGUAGE.

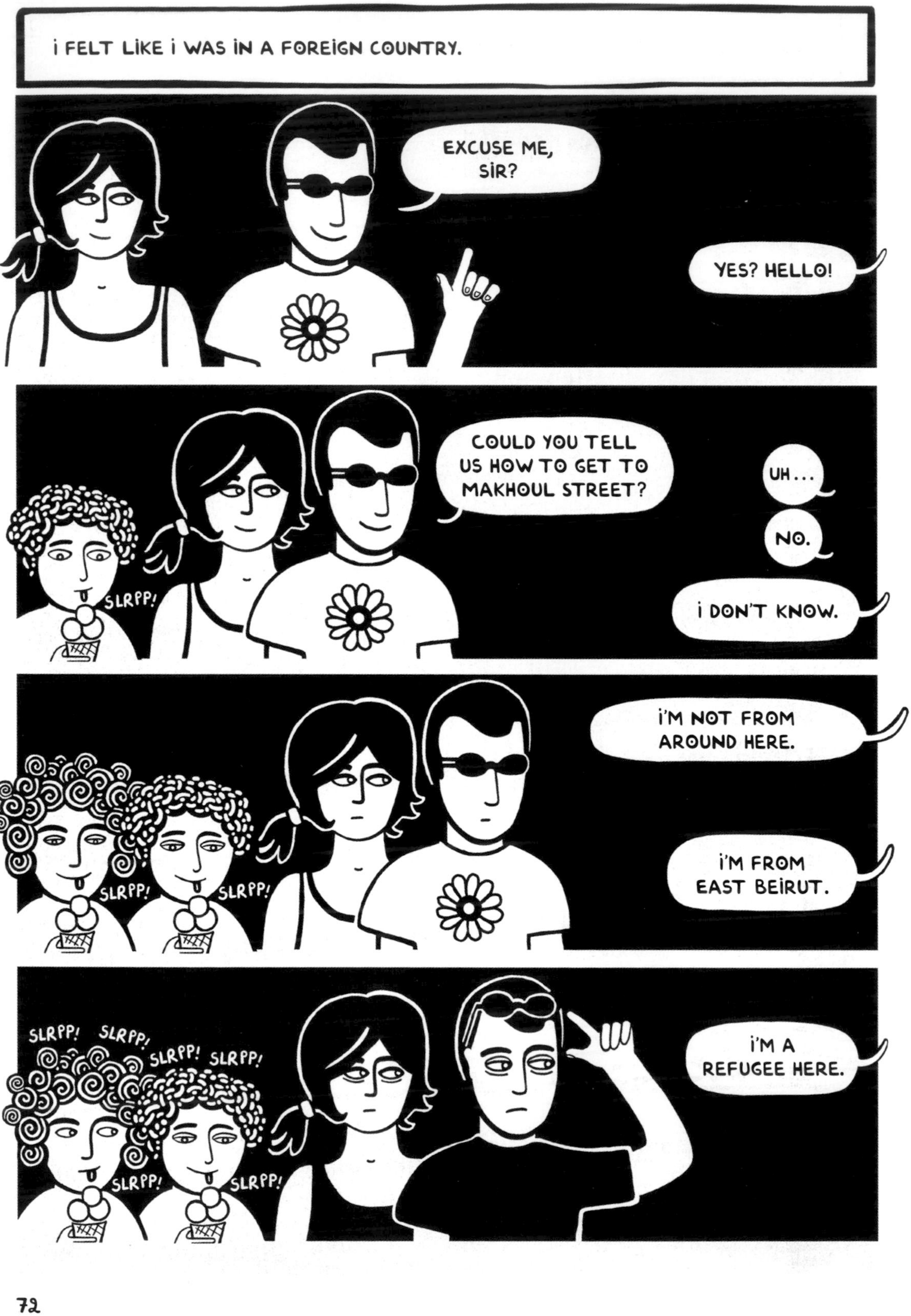
I FELT LIKE I WAS IN A FOREIGN COUNTRY.
EXCUSE ME, SIR?
YES? HELLO!
COULD YOU TELL US HOW TO GET TO MAKHOUL STREET?
SLRPP!
UH...
NO.
I DON'T KNOW.
SLRPP!
SLRPP!
I'M NOT FROM AROUND HERE.
I'M FROM EAST BEIRUT.
SLRPP! SLRPP! SLRPP! SLRPP!
SLRPP!
SLRPP!
I'M A REFUGEE HERE.

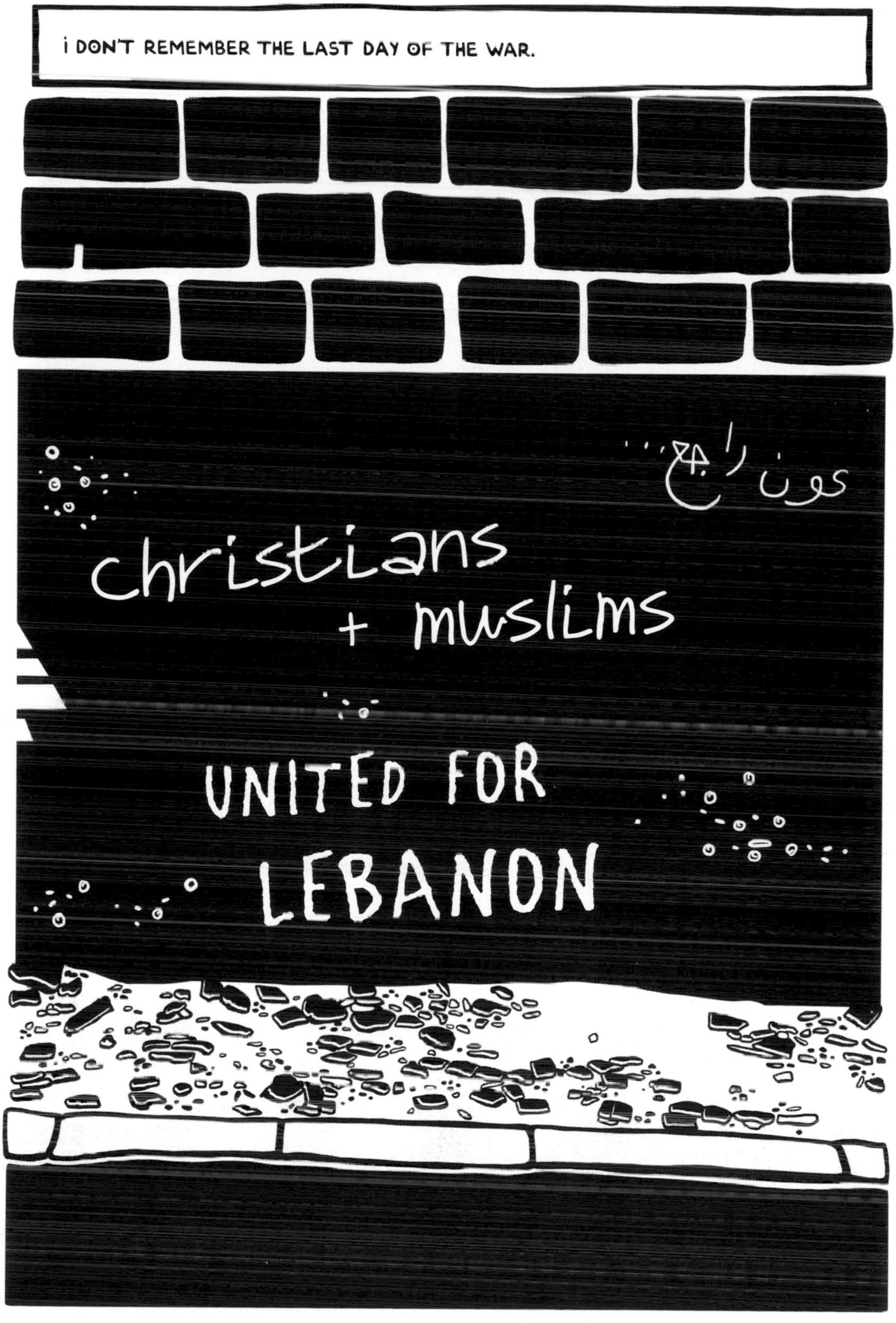
I DON'T REMEMBER THE LAST DAY OF THE WAR.
كون راجع
christians
+ muslims
UNITED FOR
LEBANON

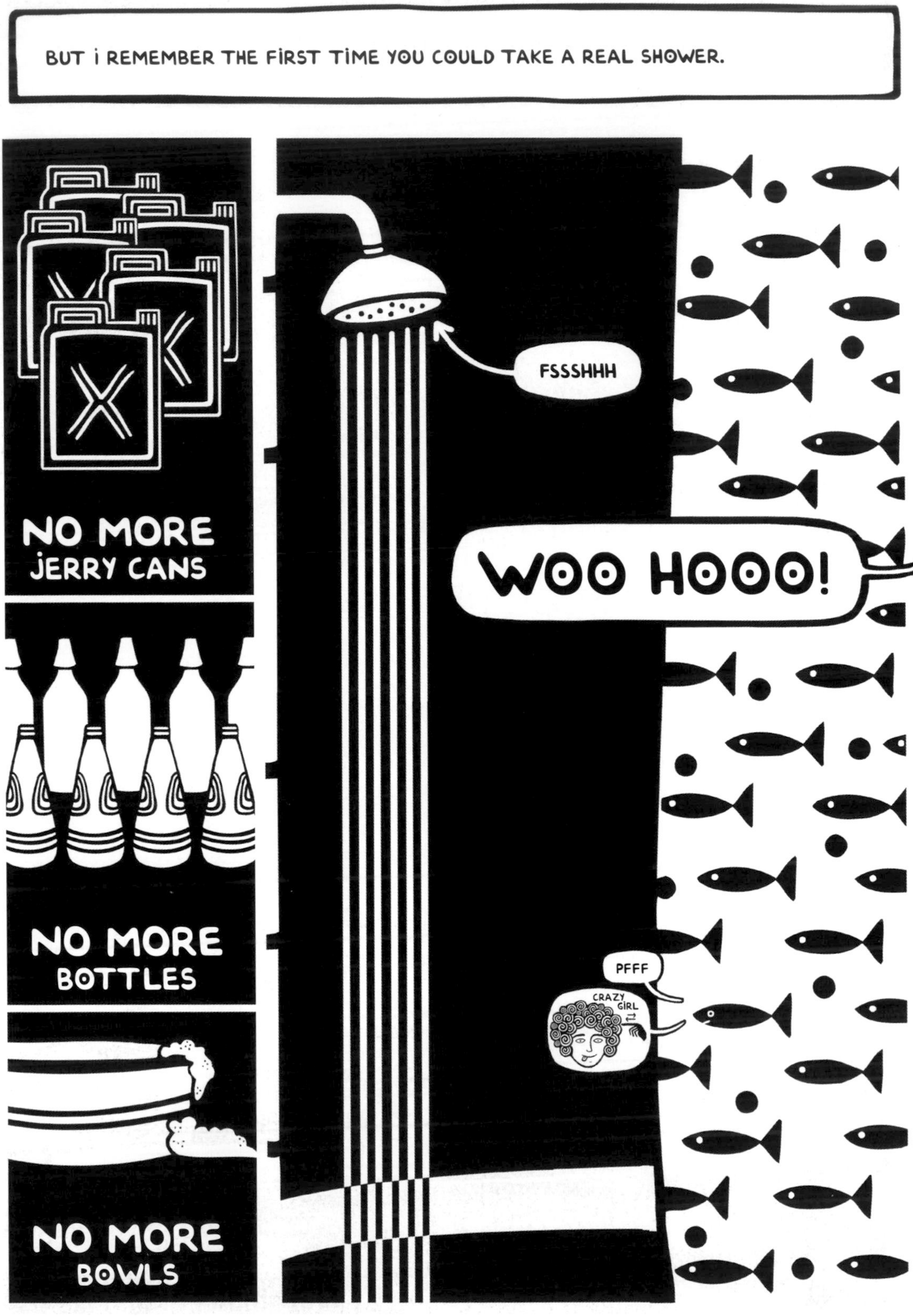
BUT i REMEMBER THE FiRST TiME YOU COULD TAKE A REAL SHOWER.
NO MORE JERRY CANS
NO MORE BOTTLES
NO MORE BOWLS
FSSSHHH
WOO HOOO!
PFFF
CRAZY GiRL

I DON'T REMEMBER THE EXACT DAY THE WALL ACROSS YOUSSEF SEMAANI STREET WAS DESTROYED.

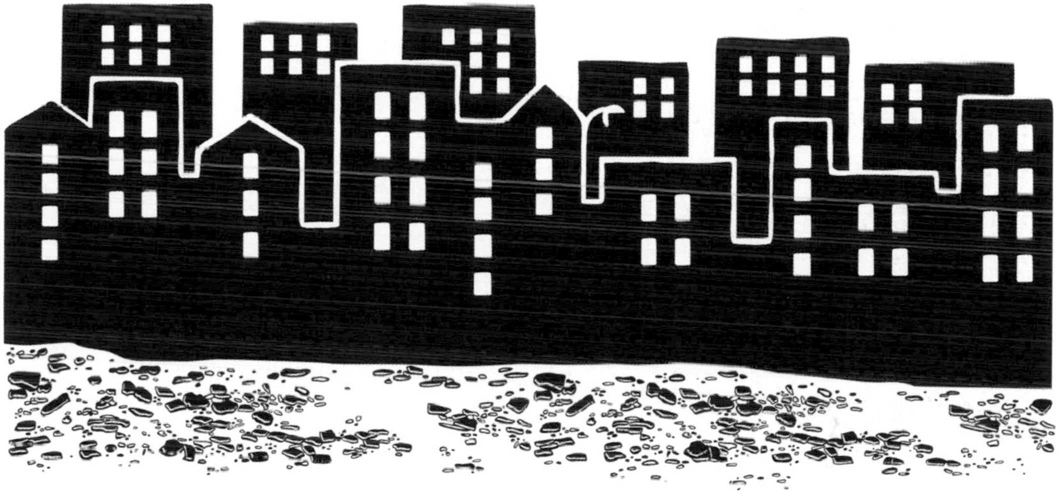

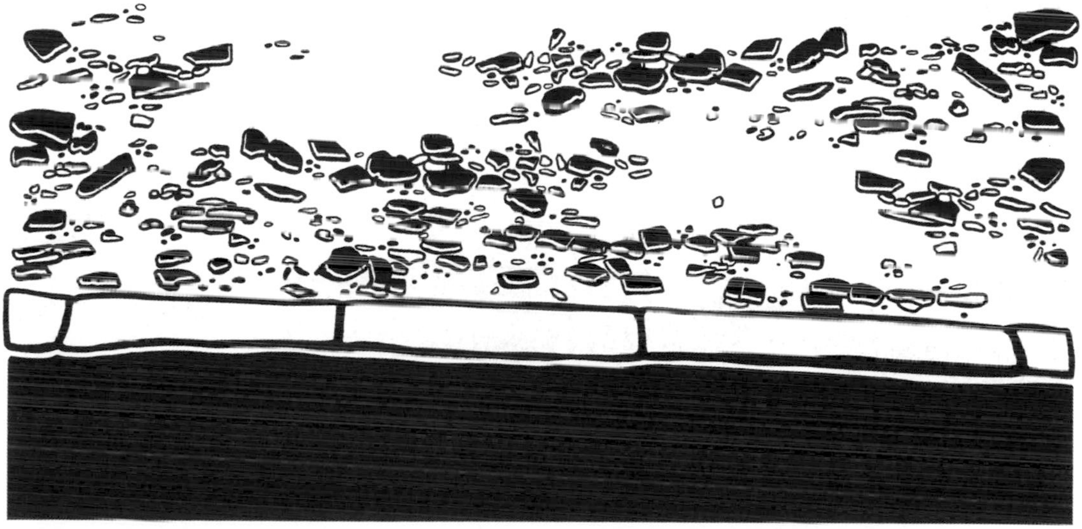

BUT I REMEMBER MY SURPRISE WHEN, TEN YEARS AFTER THE WAR ENDED, I WAS WALKING IN BEIRUT AND REALIZED THAT THE STREET ACROSS FROM WHERE I LIVED, WHICH FOR FIFTEEN YEARS HAD BEEN THE "OTHER SIDE," WAS ALSO CALLED... YOUSSEF SEMAANI STREET.

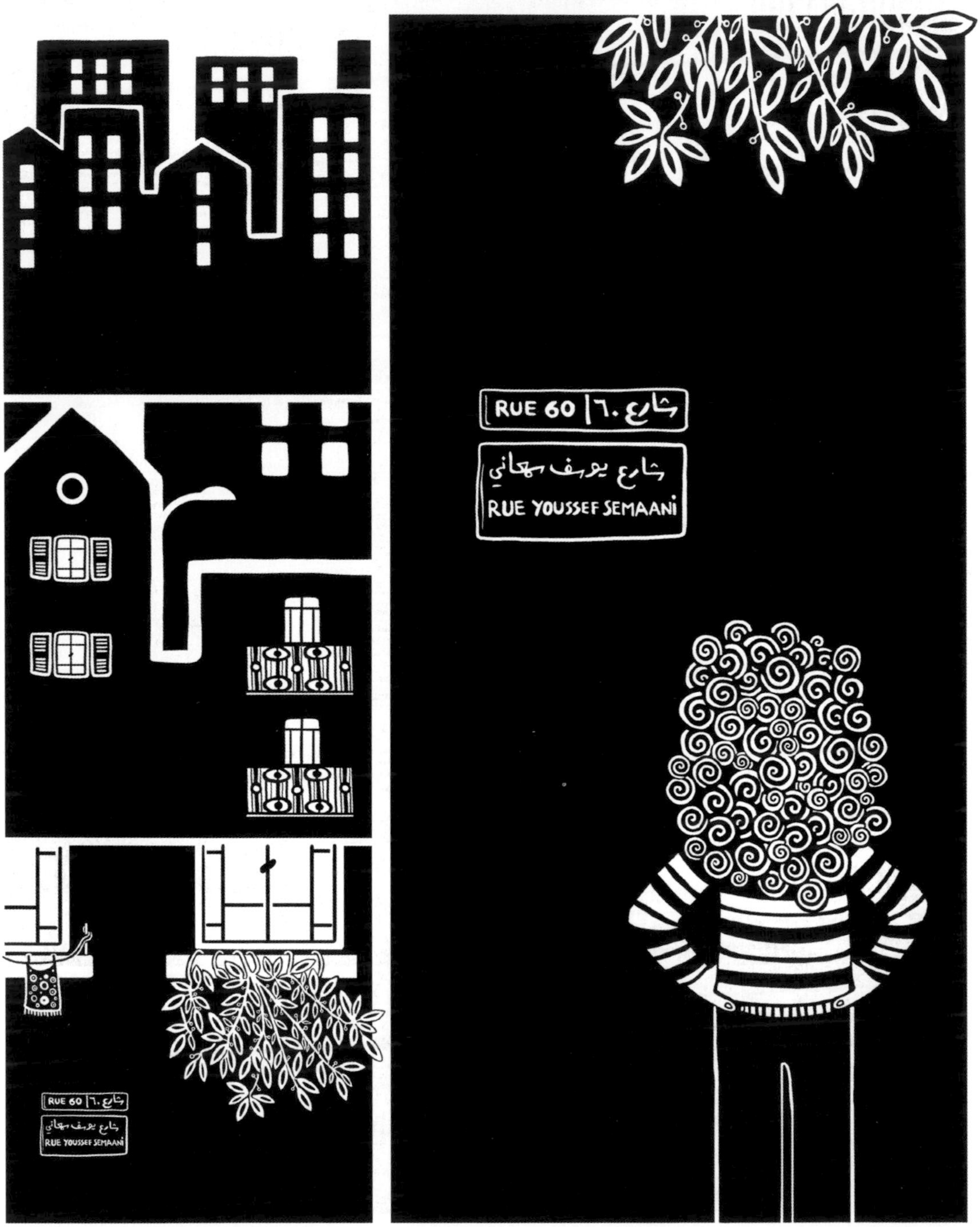

RUE 60 | شارع ٦٠
RUE YOUSSEF SEMAANI
RUE 60 | شارع ٦٠
RUE YOUSSEF SEMAANI

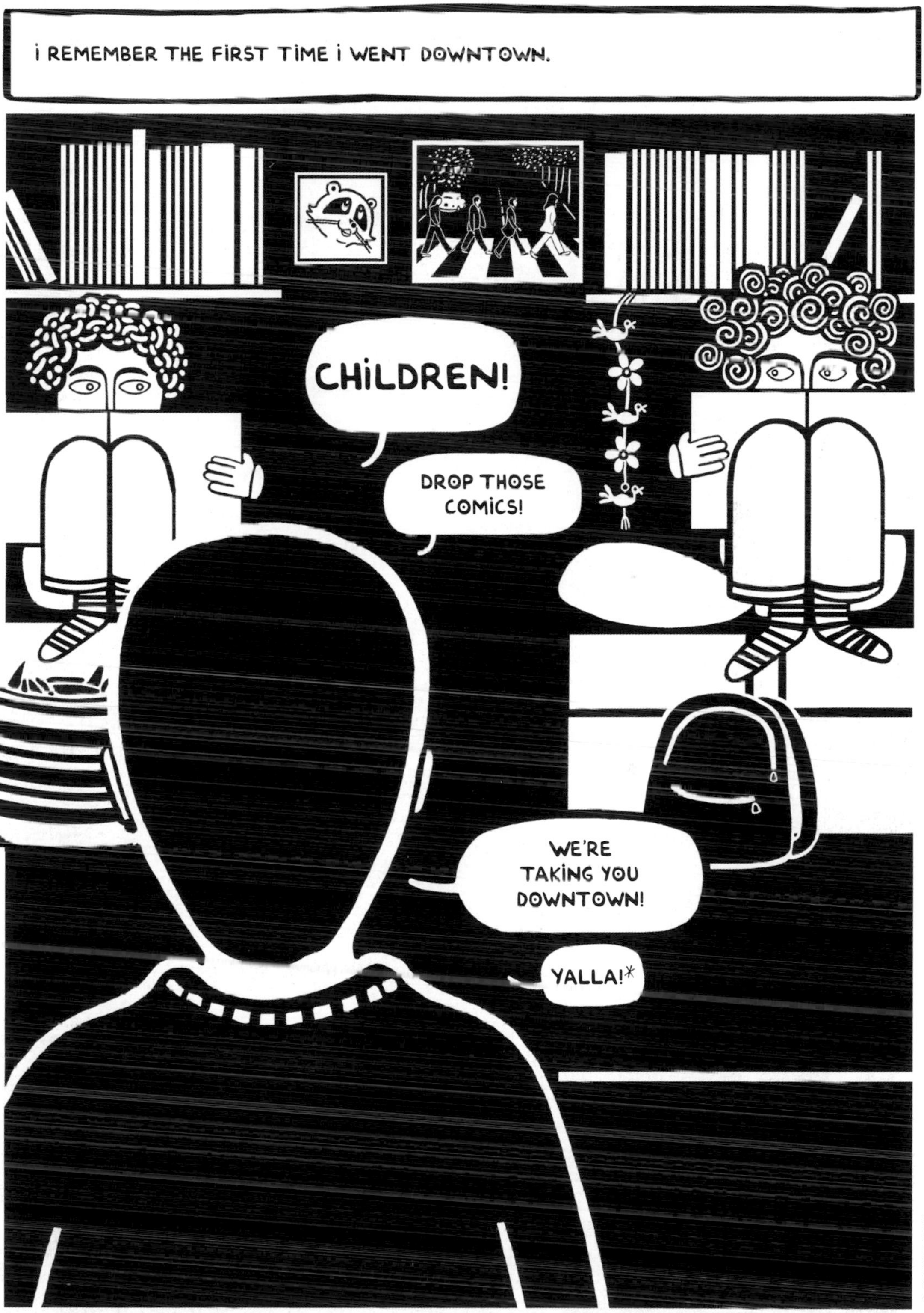
I REMEMBER THE FIRST TIME I WENT DOWNTOWN.
CHILDREN!
DROP THOSE COMICS!
WE'RE TAKING YOU DOWNTOWN!
YALLA!*

* COME ON!

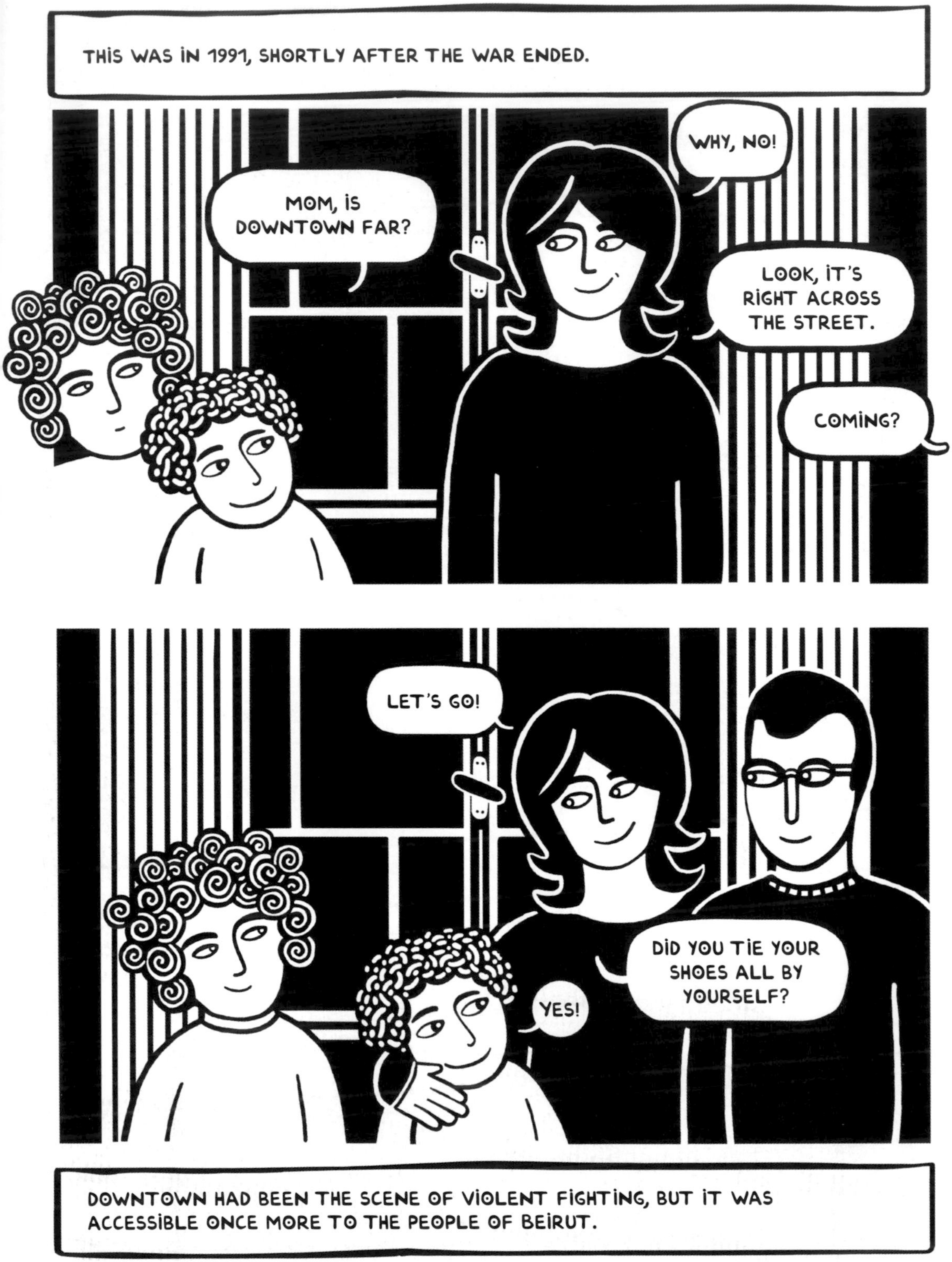
THIS WAS IN 1991, SHORTLY AFTER THE WAR ENDED.
MOM, IS DOWNTOWN FAR?
WHY, NO!
LOOK, IT'S RIGHT ACROSS THE STREET.
COMING?
LET'S GO!
DID YOU TIE YOUR SHOES ALL BY YOURSELF?
YES!
DOWNTOWN HAD BEEN THE SCENE OF VIOLENT FIGHTING, BUT IT WAS ACCESSIBLE ONCE MORE TO THE PEOPLE OF BEIRUT.

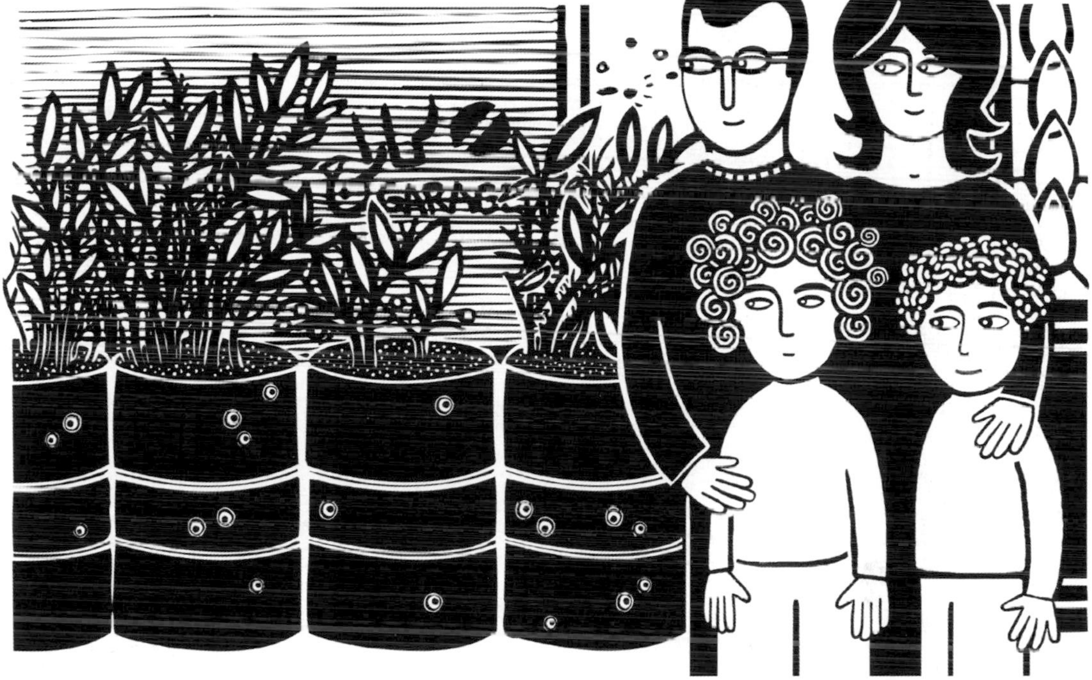

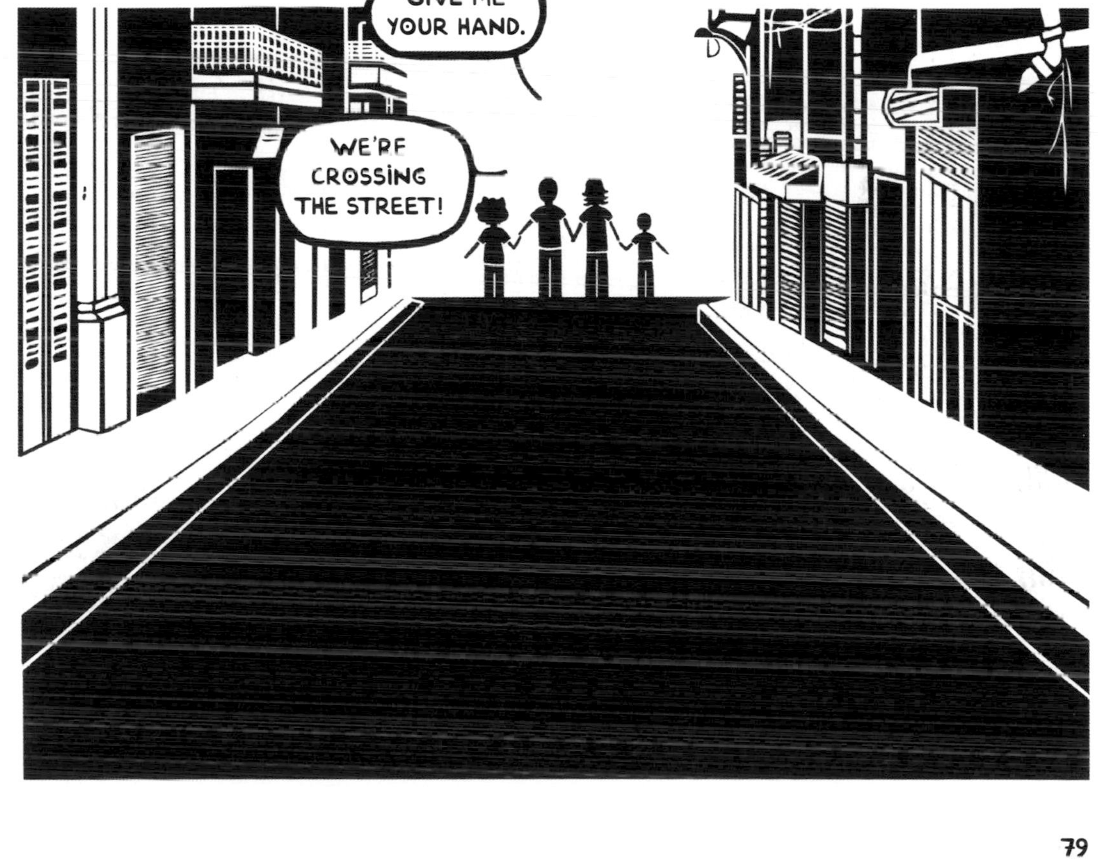
GIVE ME YOUR HAND.
WE'RE CROSSING THE STREET!

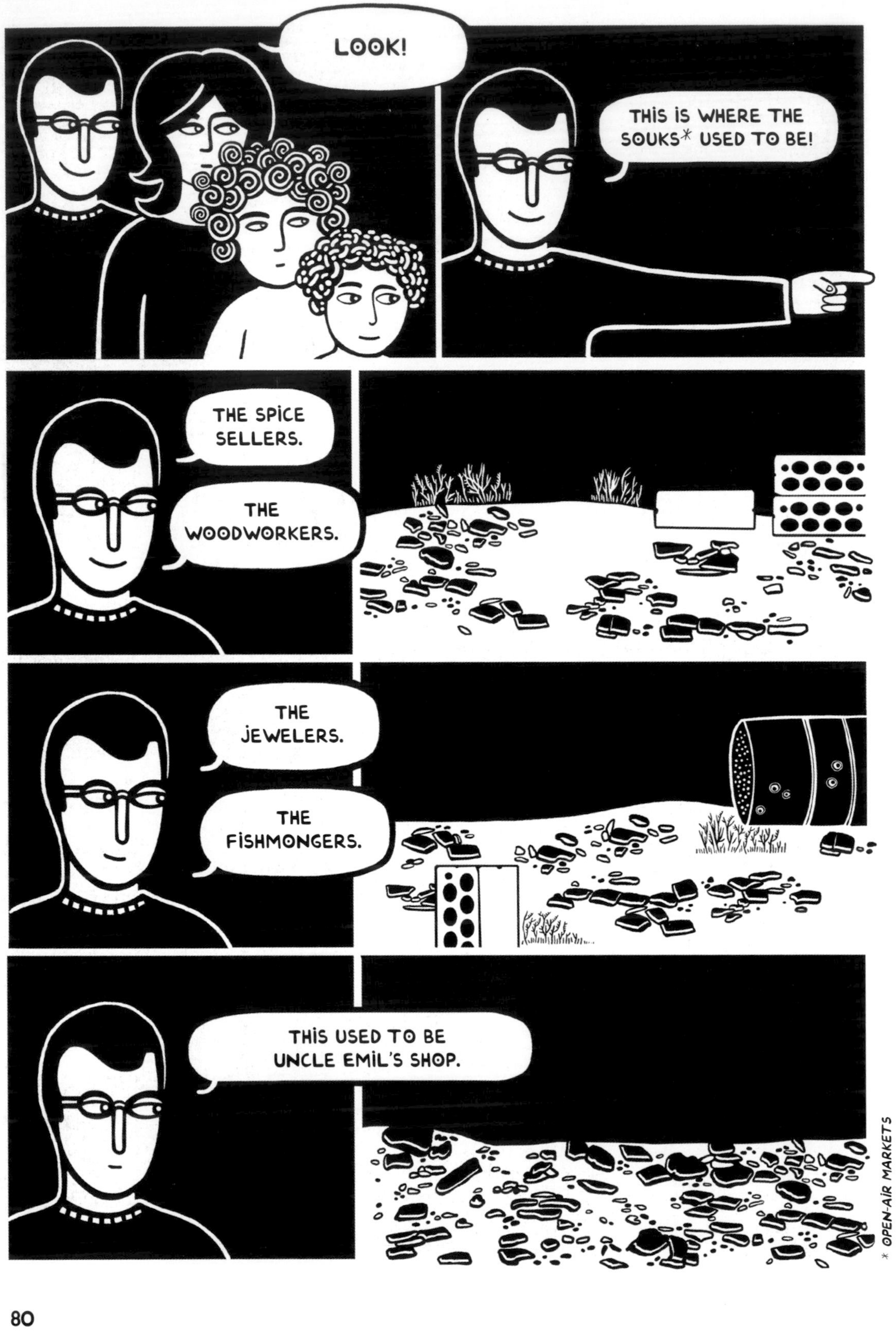
LOOK!
THIS IS WHERE THE SOUKS* USED TO BE!
THE SPICE SELLERS.
THE WOODWORKERS.
THE JEWELERS.
THE FISHMONGERS.
THIS USED TO BE UNCLE EMIL'S SHOP.

* OPEN-AIR MARKETS

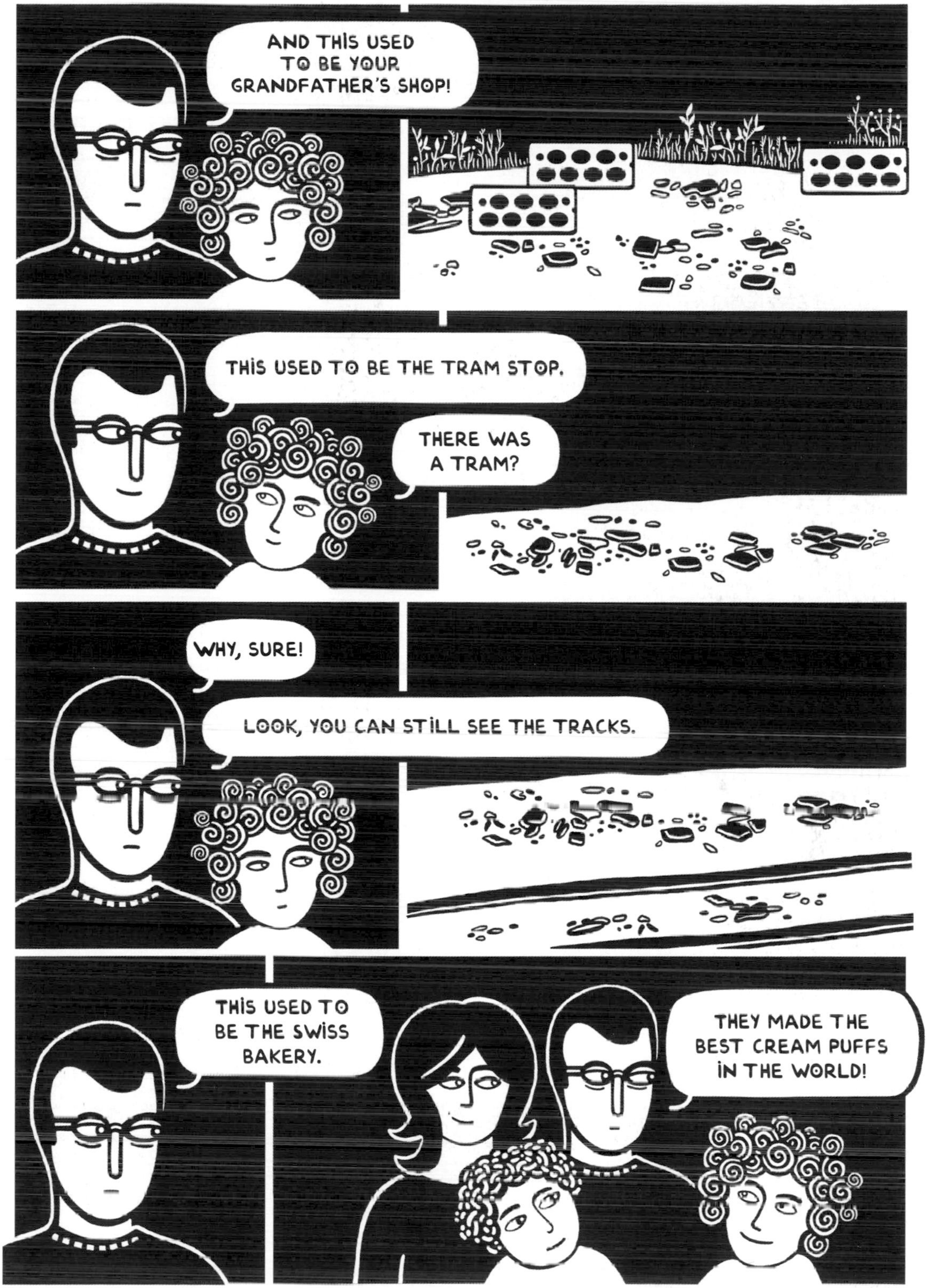
AND THIS USED TO BE YOUR GRANDFATHER'S SHOP!
THIS USED TO BE THE TRAM STOP.
THERE WAS A TRAM?
WHY, SURE!
LOOK, YOU CAN STILL SEE THE TRACKS.
THIS USED TO BE THE SWISS BAKERY.
THEY MADE THE BEST CREAM PUFFS IN THE WORLD!

I REMEMBER THAT ON OUR WAY BACK FROM DOWNTOWN, MY FATHER DIDN'T FEEL THAT WELL...

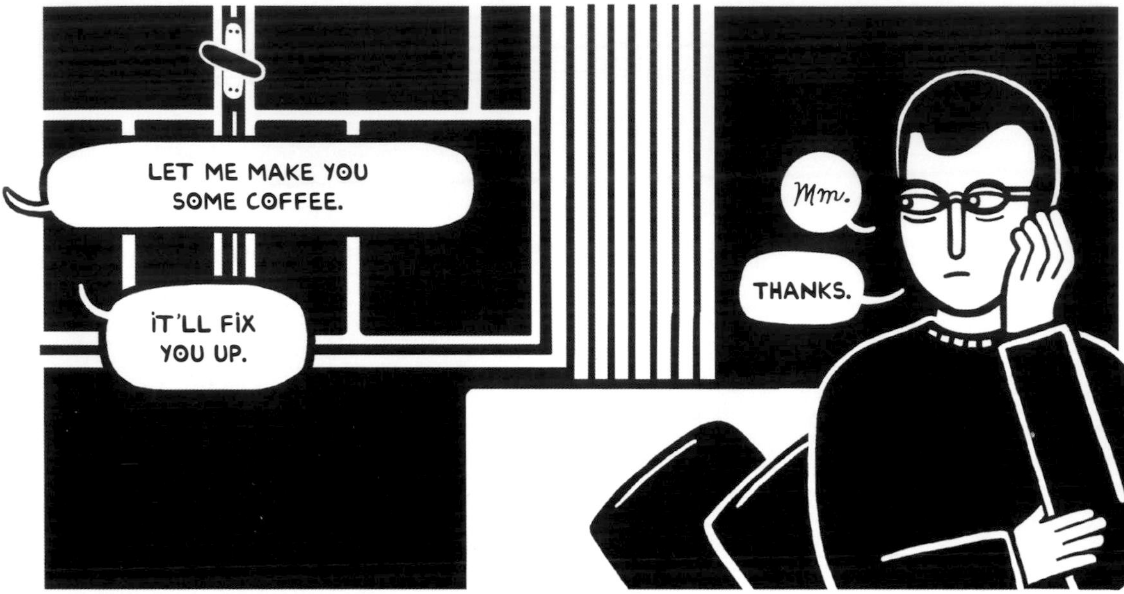
LET ME MAKE YOU SOME COFFEE.
IT'LL FIX YOU UP.
Mm.
THANKS.

...BUT MY BROTHER WAS VERY HAPPY.

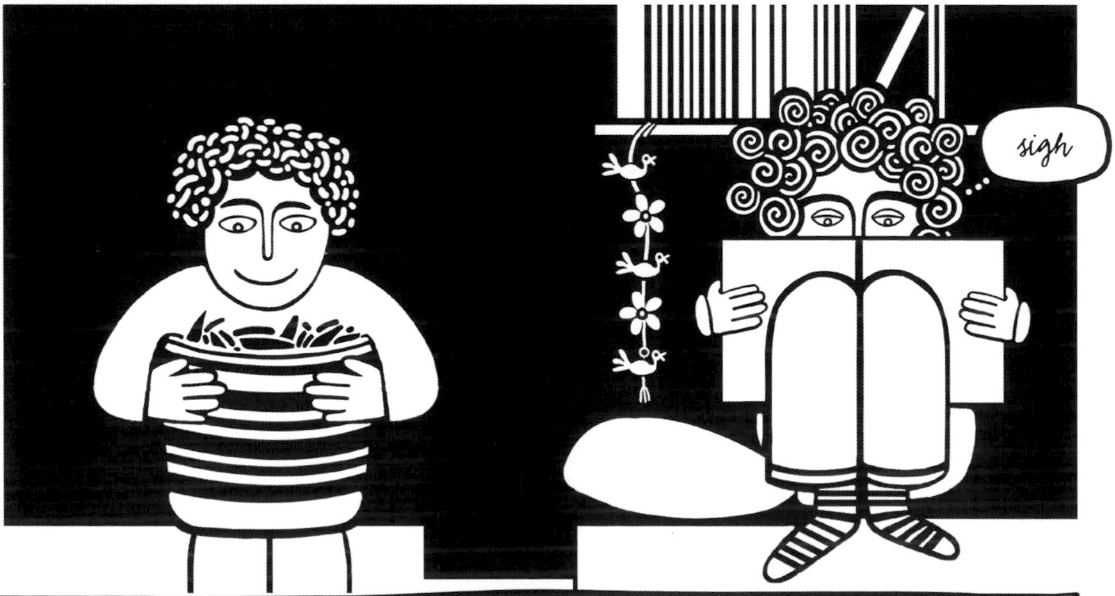
sigh

HE'D JUST GOTTEN SOME VERY UNIQUE PIECES FOR HIS COLLECTION.

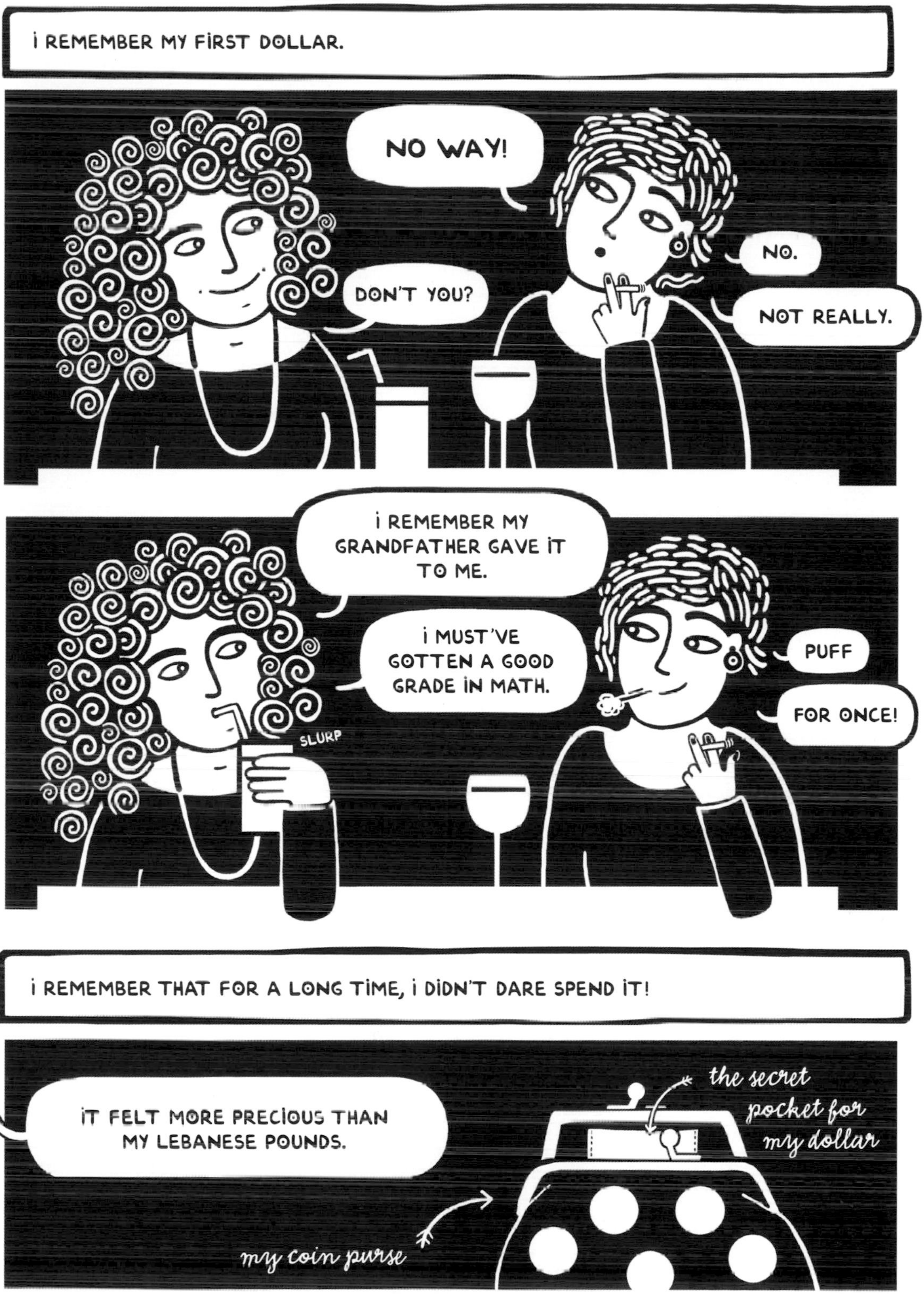
I REMEMBER MY FIRST DOLLAR.
NO WAY!
DON'T YOU?
NO.
NOT REALLY.
I REMEMBER MY GRANDFATHER GAVE IT TO ME.
I MUST'VE GOTTEN A GOOD GRADE IN MATH.
SLURP
PUFF
FOR ONCE!
I REMEMBER THAT FOR A LONG TIME, I DIDN'T DARE SPEND IT!
IT FELT MORE PRECIOUS THAN MY LEBANESE POUNDS.
the secret pocket for my dollar
my coin purse

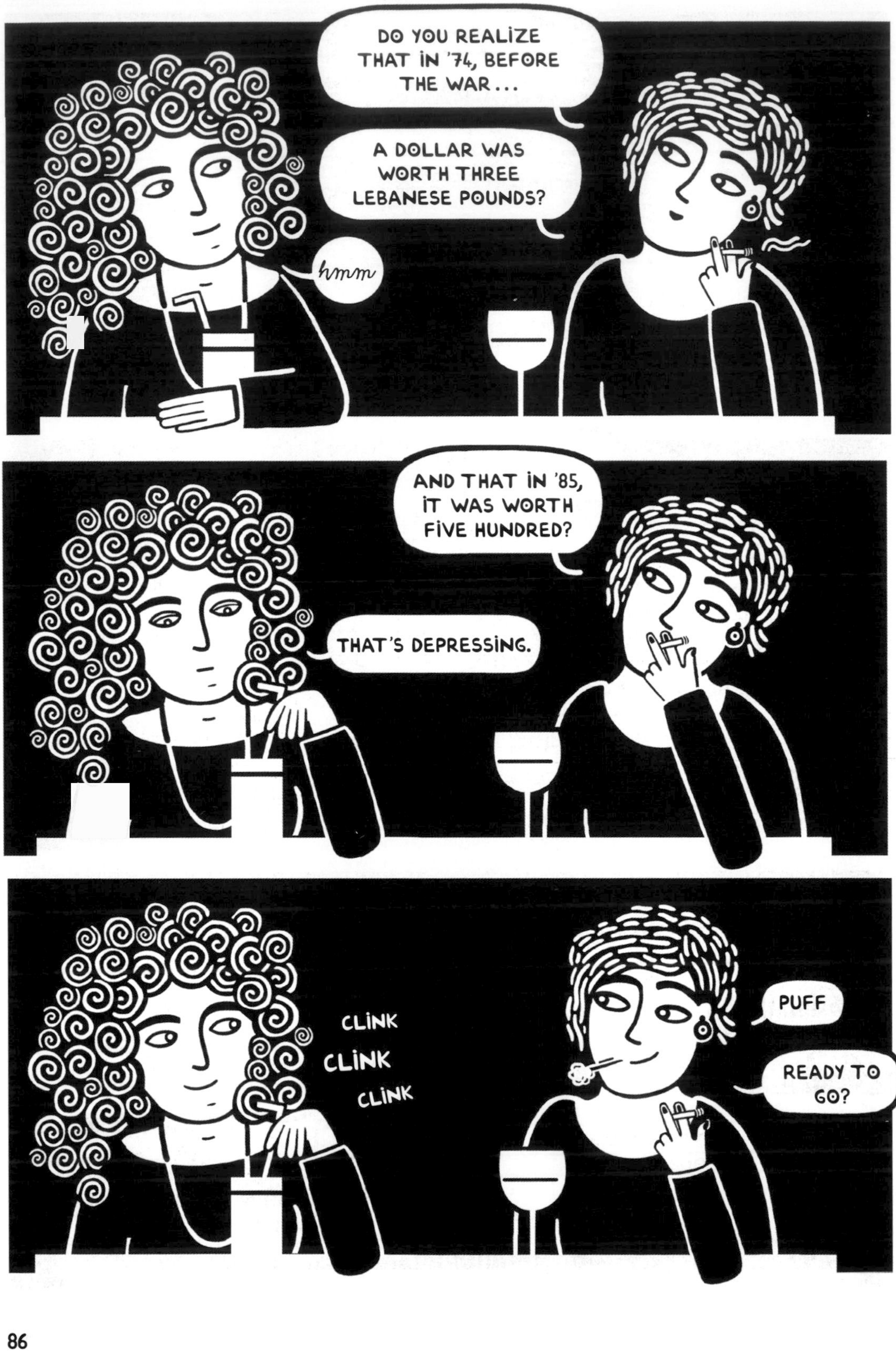
DO YOU REALIZE THAT IN '74, BEFORE THE WAR...
A DOLLAR WAS WORTH THREE LEBANESE POUNDS?
hmm
AND THAT IN '85, IT WAS WORTH FIVE HUNDRED?
THAT'S DEPRESSING.
CLINK
CLINK
CLINK
PUFF
READY TO GO?

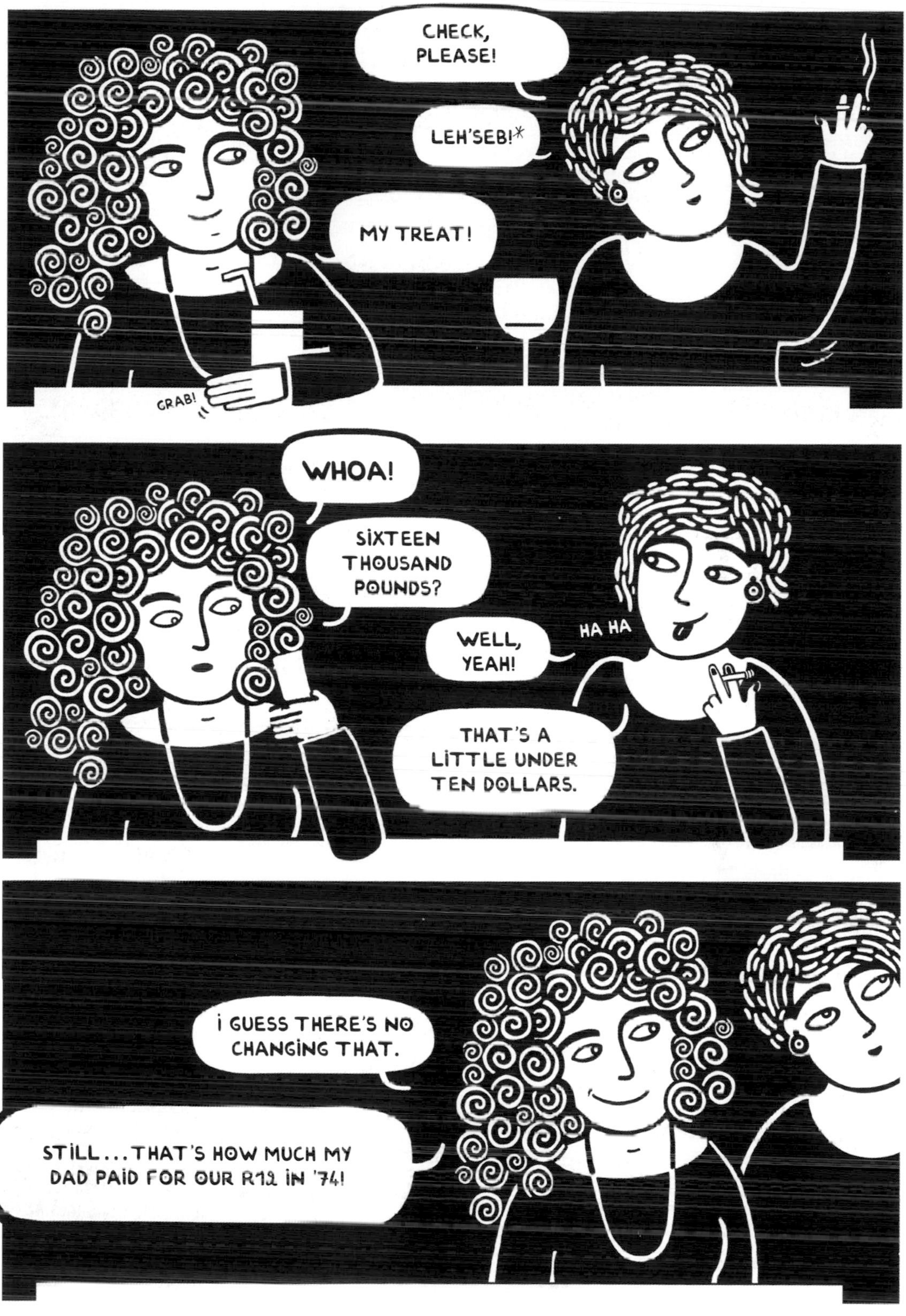
CHECK, PLEASE!
LEH'SEB!*
MY TREAT!
GRAB!
WHOA!
SIXTEEN THOUSAND POUNDS?
WELL, YEAH!
HA HA
THAT'S A LITTLE UNDER TEN DOLLARS.
I GUESS THERE'S NO CHANGING THAT.
STILL... THAT'S HOW MUCH MY DAD PAID FOR OUR R12 IN '74!

* CHECK

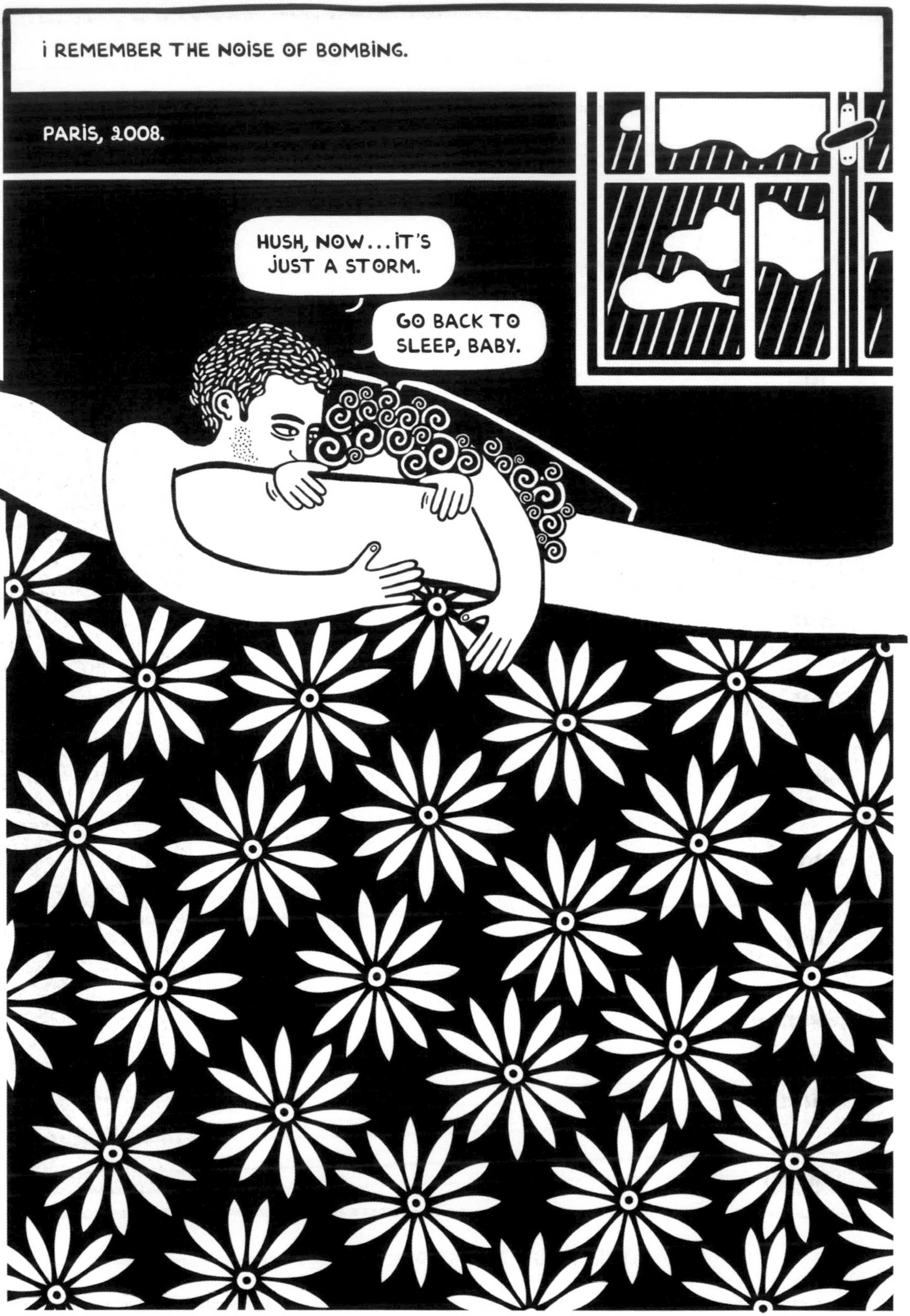
I REMEMBER THE NOISE OF BOMBING.
PARIS, 2008.
HUSH, NOW... IT'S JUST A STORM.
GO BACK TO SLEEP, BABY.

I REMEMBER JULY 2006.

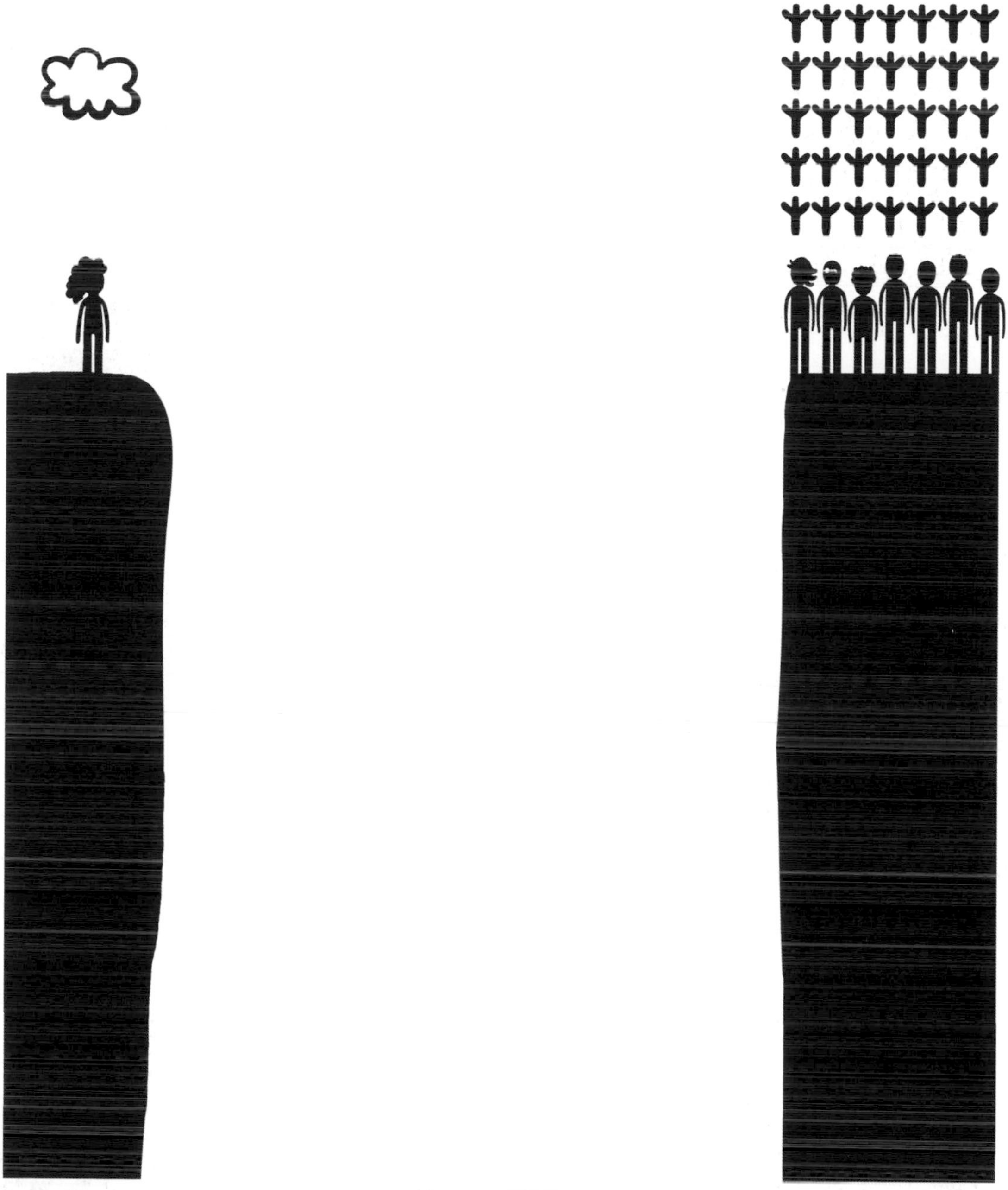

I'M IN PARIS. THEY'RE ALL OVER THERE.

JUST TWENTY YEARS EARLIER, MY BIGGEST FEAR WAS LOSING THEM.

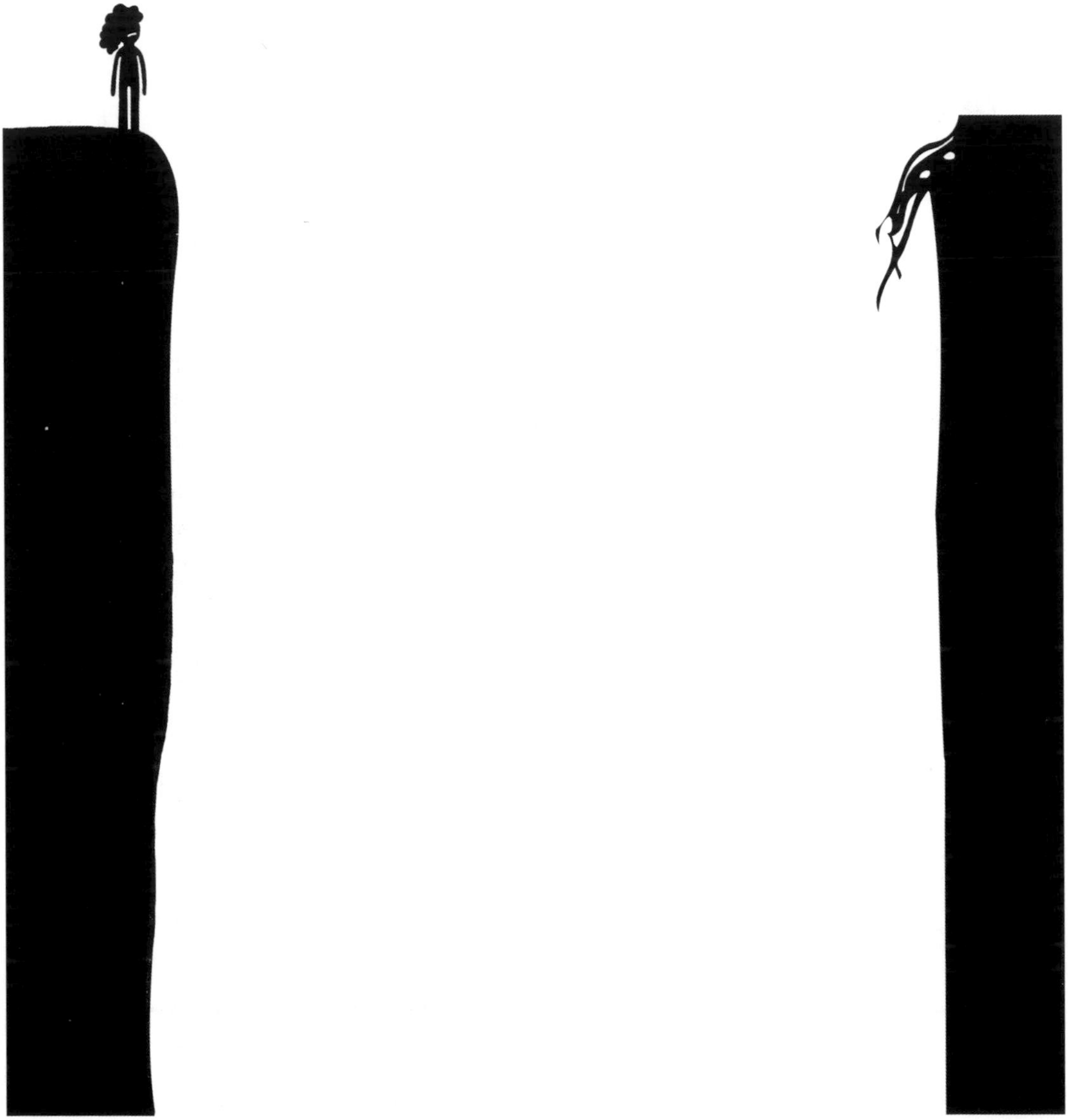

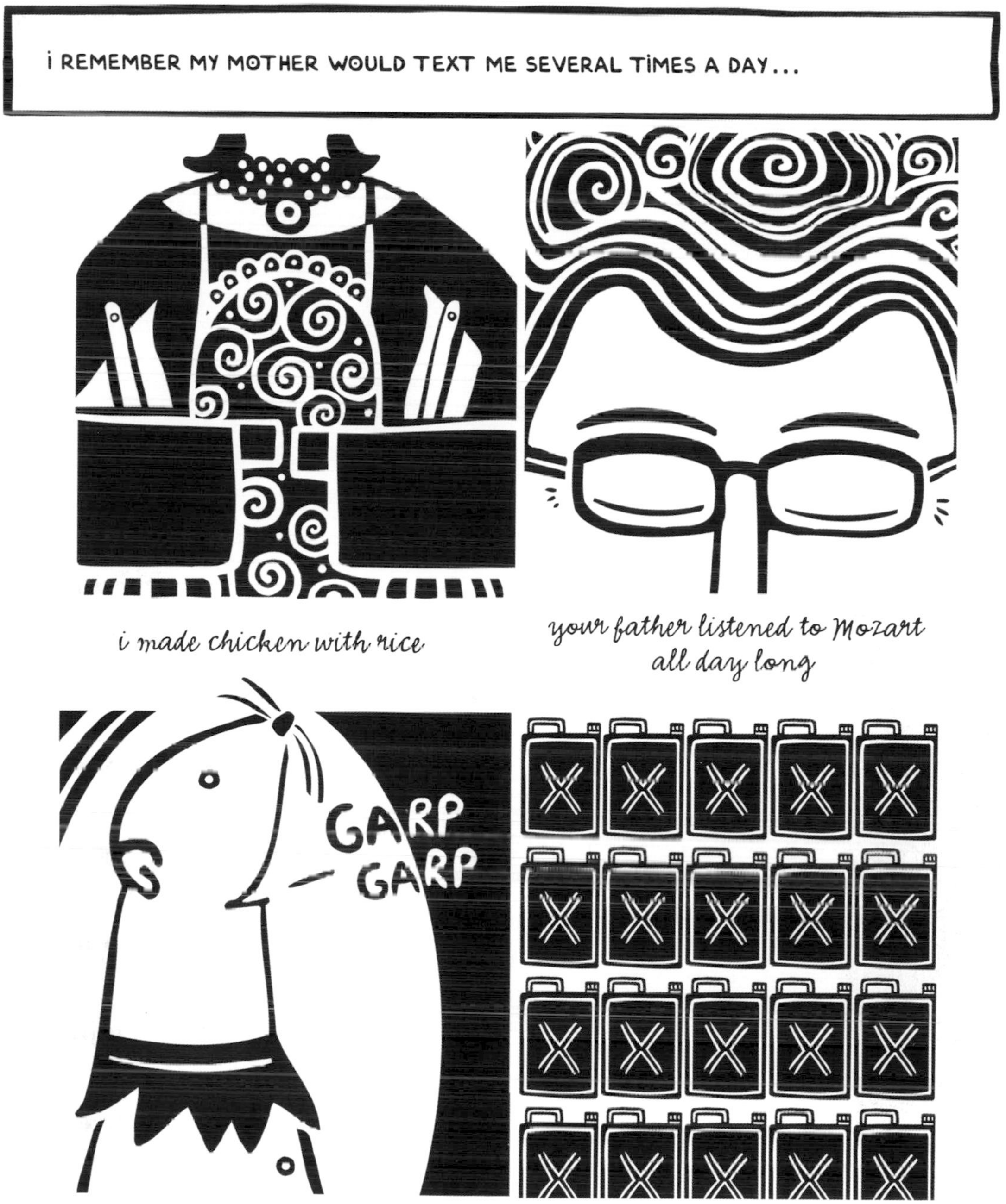
i REMEMBER MY MOTHER WOULD TEXT ME SEVERAL TiMES A DAY...
i made chicken with rice
your father listened to Mozart all day long
GARP GARP
your brother finished reading "The World According to Garp"
Chucri gave us some gas
...TO REASSURE ME.

BUT I KNOW WHAT THEY WENT THROUGH IN ALL THE TEXTS SHE DIDN'T SEND.

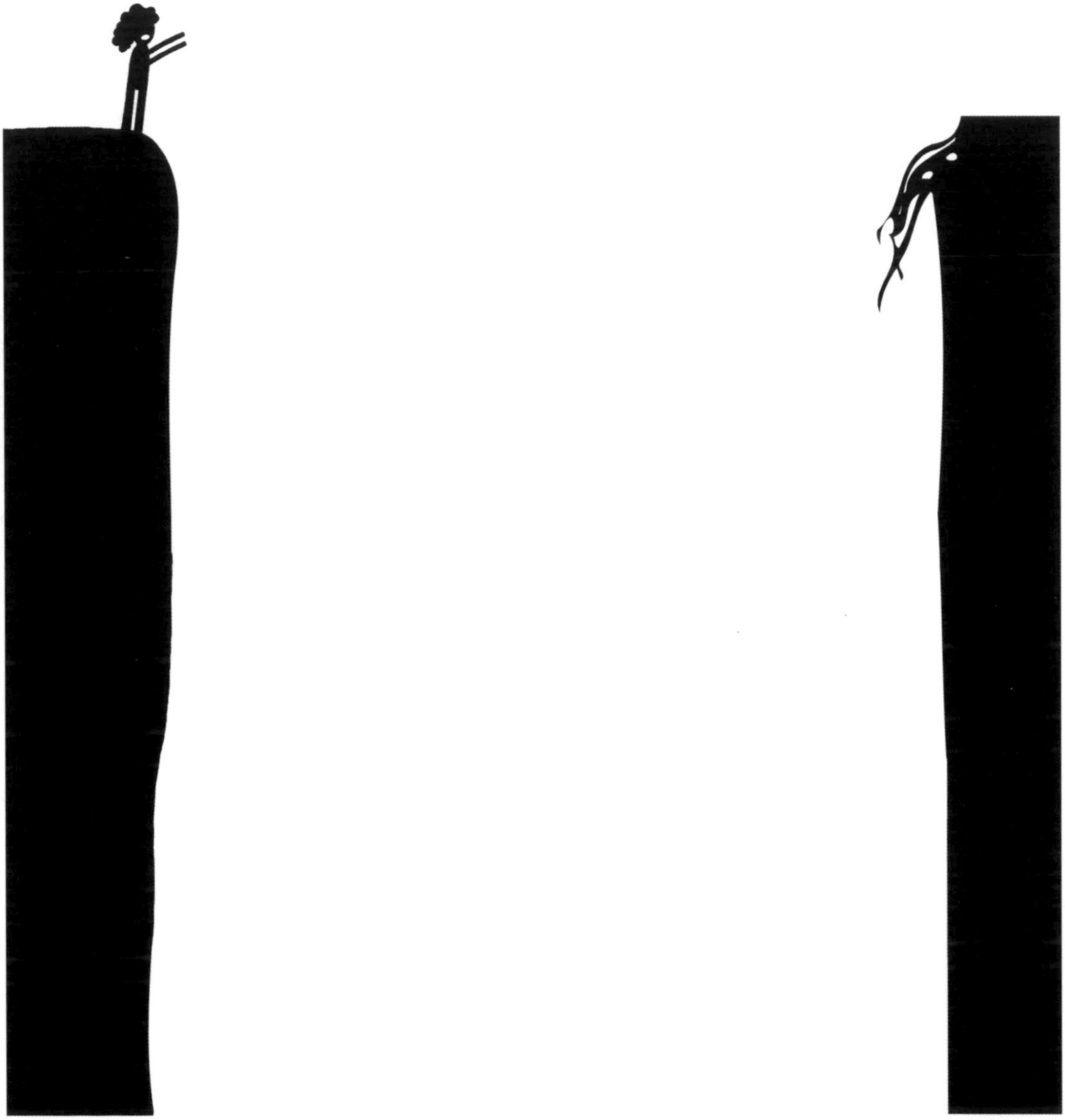

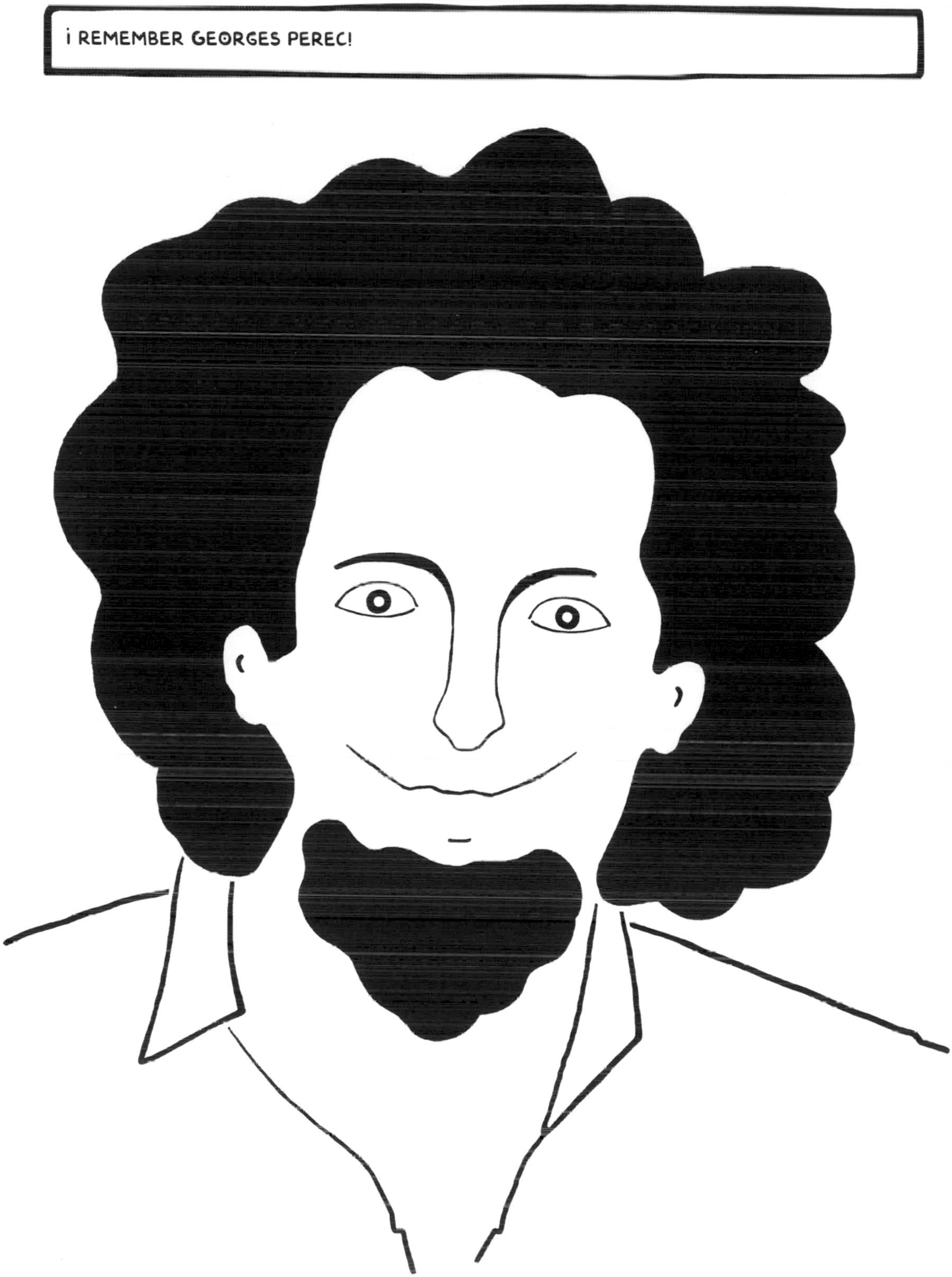
I REMEMBER GEORGES PEREC!

ABOUT THE AUTHOR

Zeina Abirached was born in Beirut in 1981 in the middle of the civil war and was ten years old when it finally ended. She studied graphic arts and commercial design at the Lebanese Academy of Fine Arts (ALBA) and in 2002 was awarded the top prize at the International Comic Book Festival in Beirut for her first graphic novel, *Beyrouth-Catharsis*. She moved to Paris in 2004, where she attended the National School of Decorative Arts. In 2006, she published her two graphic novels in French with the publisher Cambourakis, and the next year her short animated film, *Mouton* (*Sheep*), received a prize nomination during the 5th Tehran International Animation Festival.

While surfing a French online news archive, she came across a television documentary made in Beirut in 1984. The reporters were interviewing the residents of a street near the demarcation line that cut the city in two. A woman whose home had been hit by the bombings spoke a single sentence that startled her: "You know, I think maybe we're still more or less safe here."

That woman was her grandmother. At that moment, she knew she had to tell the story of their lives in Beirut.